T0113442

A tale of three cities
The 1993 Rede Lecture and related summit declarations

L. M. SINGHVI

The Rede Lecture given by
His Excellency the High Commissioner for India,
Dr L. M. Singhvi
in the Senate House, University of Cambridge,
on 30 November 1993

CAMBRIDGE
UNIVERSITY PRESS

CAMBRIDGE UNIVERSITY PRESS
Cambridge, New York, Melbourne, Madrid, Cape Town, Singapore, São Paulo

Cambridge University Press
The Edinburgh Building, Cambridge CB2 2RU, UK

Published in the United States of America by Cambridge University Press, New York

www.cambridge.org
Information on this title: www.cambridge.org/9780521578189

First published 1996

A catalogue record for this publication is available from the British Library

ISBN-13 978-0-521-57818-9 paperback
ISBN-10 0-521-57818-3 paperback

Transferred to digital printing 2005

Contents

Foreword	*page* v
Preface	vi
The Rio Declaration on Environment and Development	1
Vienna Declaration and Programme of Action	5
A Global Ethic	40
A tale of three cities: the Rede Lecture 1993	55

For the Seven Stars in my life
Kamlaji, Abhishek, Abhilasha, Anubhav, Astha,
Avishkar and Nishtha

Foreword

Nearly five centuries ago, in an era of unequalled social and political change in Europe, a leading English jurist Sir Robert Rede founded a lectureship at Cambridge University. After many changes over the years this appointment continues today as one of the most prestigious the University can offer, and provides for a leading public figure to lecture on a subject of their choice.

Dr Singhvi, whose lecture is published in this volume, could not have been a more appropriate choice, nor could his subject have been more relevant to our times. His own career – as a distinguished advocate, as a parliamentarian, as a tireless representative of his great country overseas – could not have equipped him better for his theme. And the theme itself is indeed a compelling one. Like Sir Robert Rede himself, but on a vastly larger stage, Dr Singhvi has experienced the many contending pressures and opportunities which our own era too has seen as it faces such dramatic change. This is a great and challenging topic and, as will be seen on what follows, it has found an inspired author more than equal to his task.

Sir David Williams

Preface

I was privileged to be invited by the Vice-Chancellor of the University of Cambridge to deliver the Rede Lecture in 1993. I was at once daunted and inspired by the antiquity of Sir Robert Rede's endowment which goes back to the first quarter of the sixteenth century, and the dazzling eminence of my predecessors, many of whom have been living legends in their time and age. I was also spurred as well as constrained by the pressure and paucity of time.

In my quest for the theme of my lecture, my thoughts turned to the three great contemporary themes of Environment, Human Rights and the Fundamental Unity of the Religions of the World which have inspired me for many decades and have commanded my moral and intellectual allegiance. These three themes claimed particularly heightened attention of the world in 1992–3. It transpired that three major world conferences were held in Rio, Vienna and Chicago on these themes during 1992–3. I was intimately involved with several pre-UNCED conferences and actively participated in the conferences in Vienna and Chicago. The caption 'A Tale of Three Cities' obviously promised more than I could deliver in a single lecture. My tale of three cities is meant only to be a short synoptic story of three major contemporary concerns which loom larger than life upon the horizons of future.

I confess I am generally inclined to view large global conferences with a certain mental reservation even though one must not fail to recognise the catalytic role and opinion-building impact of such conferences. The three conferences in Rio, Vienna and Chicago did not escape my misgivings, but I felt and found that the three conferences were substantive and significant milestones of shared concern throughout the world and did, in fact, achieve certain notable results with considerable potential for good. They did identify the problems as well as their causes. They articulated the collective aspirations of the world community. They suggested many practical solutions and produced balanced doctrinal formulations. Most importantly, they provided opportunities for cross-cultural dialogue and interaction. They also achieved a considerable measure of consensus. With certain unavoidable shortcomings of international conferences, the conferences in Rio, Vienna and Chicago did provide a new emphasis on restraint and responsibility in the use of the world's finite resources, on population control and on prevention of environmental degradation; a new recognition of the primary importance of a sense of human obligations of world citizenship; and a new acceptance of an affirmative concept of mutual tolerance, understanding, acceptance and celebration of the diverse religions of the world through dialogue.

I regard the new beginnings made at Rio, Vienna and Chicago modest but momentous and meaningful. They did not achieve all that could have been and should have been achieved but they were, undoubtedly, pioneering pace-setting initiatives which gave the peoples and the governments of the world a clearer sense of direction and a practical agenda for reflection and action. Unfortunately, those who sulk and wallow in their disappointment invariably fail to see the strides of progress.

I entered the portals of the Senate House in the University of Cambridge to deliver the Lecture with the utmost trepidation even though the presence of my distinguished friend Professor Sir David Williams by my side was reassuring. The gods were kind to me and so were the dons and students who came to the lecture. The distinguished audience was patient and polite. I felt flattered and encouraged when the Vice-Chancellor, Professor Sir David Williams, very kindly suggested that the Lecture ought to be published. I am beholden to him for writing a friendly Foreword to this publication.

For a while I toyed with the idea of elaborating my thoughts and

Preface

enlarging the lecture, providing footnotes and giving it a more respectable academic appearance, but I soon found it less and less feasible. As a practical measure, I settled for appending the basic documents which came out of the three conferences. I hope those documents will help to redeem and make up for the brevity of the text of my Lecture. I was prompted to opt for brevity by my conviction that it is unforgivably inconsiderate to transgress the tolerance limits of one's audience.

I am convinced that our ecological concerns have to be addressed at all levels, global, national, local and individual and an all-out effort has to be made to give our environmental agenda the highest primacy and priority. The tide of the culture of consumerism has to be stemmed and reversed. The so-called developed world must develop a greater sense of ecological accountability. The highly 'developed' and the less developed world must cooperate to initiate and implement an equitable programme. We must learn to reduce our wants and to practise moderation. World population has to be stabilised and reduced over a period of time. Patterns of consumption and models of economic growth have to be modified. Sustainable development is no longer to be regarded merely as a fashionable phrase; it has to be implemented as an immediate imperative. Wastages have to be drastically reduced. Resources must be renewed and recycled. Science and technology must concentrate on environmental problems and their solutions. Above all, I consider Environment as a collective human right of humankind and any persistent pattern of ecocide as a gross violation of human right. For nearly two decades, I have pleaded for a Third Covenant on Environment broadly similar to the International Covenant on Political and Civil Rights and the International Covenant on Social, Economic and Cultural Rights. I believe that the time for that idea in one form or the other has come and I hope that its period of gestation would not be unduly long.

The UN Conference on Human Rights in Vienna moved in the direction of consolidating the human rights jurisprudence and practice. Hastening gently, the UN Conference faced and resolved to

viii

a certain extent the extremely divisive issue of the universality of human rights versus cultural diversities of different societies with different perceptions of human rights norms and at different stages of development. It also paved the way for the establishment of the institution of UN Human Rights Commissioner. It made the peoples of the world aware of the perils of intolerance, discrimination, fanaticism, xenophobia and terrorism and provided for vital human rights safeguards. It gave a more explicit and pronounced recognition to the concept of the human rights to development in a holistic perspective and achieved a greater sense of reconciliation between the need for economic development and the respect for human rights. Environmental rights as well as rights of women and children became core issues. The Vienna Declaration made it conceptually clear that civil and political rights are so inextricably intertwined with social, economic and cultural rights that there has to be a constant concordance and corresponding contextualisation between them providing a viable basis for a dynamic relationship between human needs, human rights and human obligations in an integrated framework.

The Centennial Parliament of World's Religions reflected the ethical imperatives of our embattled world. The Chicago Declaration Towards A Global Ethic spoke of the world in agony and the depth, urgency and pervasiveness of the pain of humankind, the abuses of the Earth's ecosystems, the poverty that stifles life's potential, the disregard for justice. It condemned the social disarray of the nations, the disregard for justice which pushes citizens to the margin, the anarchy overtaking our communities and the insane death of children from violence. In particular, the Declaration condemned aggression and hatred in the name of religion. It declared with hope and optimism that this agony need not be because the basis for an ethic already existed and it offered the possibility of a better order which would lead individuals away from despair and societies away from chaos.

The Declaration also affirmed that a common set of core values was found in the teachings of the religions which formed the basis of a global ethic. It reiterated that though this truth was already known, but it had yet to be lived in heart and action. It asserted that there was an irrevocable, unconditional norm for all areas of life, for families and communities, for races, nations and religions.

It declared the interdependence of one and all, based on the principle of respect for the community of living beings, for people, animals and plants, and for the preservation of Earth, air, water and soil. In unambiguous terms, it declared that the people of the world must take individual responsibility for all that they do. They must accept that all their decisions, actions, and omissions to act have consequences. It resolved to sink narrow differences for the cause of world community, practising a culture of solidarity and relatedness. It pledged the commitment of the people of the world to a culture of non-violence, respect, justice and peace, and the commitment not to oppress, injure, torture or kill other human beings, forsaking violence as a means of settling differences and to strive for a just social and economic order in which everyone has an equal chance to reach full potential as a human being. Implicit in the Declaration was a realisation that unless the world has a spiritual rebirth, civilisation is doomed. At Chicago, we may not have succeeded in building a new spiritual interfaith cathedral but we did succeed in establishing the foundation of hope. I would neither be so naive as to expect a new millennium of amity, harmony and brotherhood around the corner in a world free of strife and tension nor am I prepared to yield to modern and post-modernist cynicism and despairing cacophony. I believe my Tale of Three Cities tells us that we have a chance to rebuild human societies on the principles which have been formulated at the three world conferences on a widely accepted consensual basis. Much will now depend on how we handle the concerns which were at the heart of the three conferences held in Rio, Vienna and Chicago and how the principles formulated at these conferences are acted upon globally and locally. In my critique and in my hope rests my justification for the Lecture and its publication.

An acknowledgement of my thankful appreciation is particularly due to Mr D. K. Singh and Mr A. Kannan without whose invaluable assistance, which goes far beyond the call of duty, the manuscript text of my lecture could not have graduated into its present form.

The Rio Declaration on Environment and Development

The United Nations Conference on Environment and Development, having met at Rio de Janeiro from 3 to 14 June 1992, reaffirming the Declaration of the United Nations Conference on the Human Environment, adopted at Stockholm on 16 June 1972, and seeking to build upon it, with the goal of establishing a new and equitable global partnership through the creation of new levels of cooperation among States, key sectors of societies and people, working towards international agreements which respect the interests of all and protect the integrity of the global environmental and developmental system, recognizing the integral and interdependent nature of the Earth, our home, proclaims that:

Principle 1 Human beings are at the centre of concerns for sustainable development. They are entitled to a healthy and productive life in harmony with nature.

Principle 2 States have, in accordance with the Charter of the United Nations and the principles of international law, the sovereign right to exploit their own resources pursuant to their own environmental and developmental policies, and the responsibility to ensure that activities within their jurisdiction or control do not cause damage to the environment of other States or of areas beyond the limits of national jurisdiction.

Principle 3 The right to development must be fulfilled so as to equitably meet developmental and environmental needs of present and future generations.

Principle 4 In order to achieve sustainable development, environmental protection shall constitute an integral part of the development process and cannot be considered in isolation from it.

Principle 5 All States and all people shall cooperate in the essential task of eradicating poverty as an indispensable requirement for sustainable development, in order to decrease the disparities in standards of living and better meet the needs of the majority of the people of the world.

Principle 6 The special situation and needs of developing countries, particularly the least developed and those most environmentally vulnerable, shall be given special priority. International actions in the field of environment and development should also address the interests and needs of all countries.

Principle 7 States shall cooperate in a spirit of global partnership to conserve, protect and restore the health and integrity of the Earth's ecosystem. In view of the different contributions to global environmental degradation, States have common but differentiated responsibilities. The developed countries acknowledge the responsibility that they bear in the international pursuit of sustainable development in view of the pressures their societies place on the global environment and of the technologies and financial resources they command.

Principle 8 To achieve sustainable development and a higher quality of life for all people, States should reduce and eliminate unsustainable patterns of production and consumption and promote appropriate demographic policies.

Principle 9 States should cooperate to strengthen endogenous capacity-building for sustainable development by improving scientific understanding through exchanges of scientific and technological knowledge, and by enhancing the development, adaptation, diffusion and transfer of technologies, including new and innovative technologies.

Principle 10 Environmental issues are best handled with the participation of all concerned citizens, at the relevant level. At the national level, each individual shall have appropriate access to information concerning the environment that is held by public authorities, including information on hazardous materials and activities in their communities, and the opportunity to participate in decision-making processes. States shall facilitate and encourage public awareness and participation by making information widely available. Effective access to judicial and administrative proceedings, including redress and remedy, shall be provided.

Principle 11 States shall enact effective environmental legislation. Environmental standards, management objectives and priorities should reflect the environmental and developmental context to which they apply. Standards applied by some countries may be inappropriate and of unwarranted economic and social cost to other countries, in particular developing countries.

The Rio Declaration

Principle 12 States should cooperate to promote a supportive and open international economic system that would lead to economic growth and sustainable development in all countries, to better address the problems of environmental degradation. Trade policy measures for environmental purposes should not constitute a means of arbitrary or unjustifiable discrimination or a disguised restriction on international trade. Unilateral actions to deal with environmental challenges outside the jurisdiction of the importing country should be avoided. Environmental measures addressing transboundary or global environmental problems should, as far as possible, be based on an international consensus.

Principle 13 States shall develop national law regarding liability and compensation for the victims of pollution and other environmental damage. States shall also cooperate in an expeditious and more determined manner to develop further international law regarding liability and compensation for adverse effects of environmental damage caused by activities within their jurisdiction or control to areas beyond their jurisdiction.

Principle 14 States should effectively cooperate to discourage or prevent the relocation and transfer to other States of any activities and substances that cause severe environmental degradation or are found to be harmful to human health.

Principle 15 In order to protect the environment, the precautionary approach shall be widely applied by States according to their capabilities. Where there are threats of serious or irreversible damage, lack of full scientific certainty shall not be used as a reason for postponing cost-effective measures to prevent environmental degradation.

Principle 16 National authorities should endeavour to promote the internalization of environmental costs and the use of economic instruments, taking into account the approach that the polluter should, in principle, bear the cost of pollution, with due regard to the public interest and without distorting international trade and investment.

Principle 17 Environmental impact assessment, as a national instrument, shall be undertaken for proposed activities that are likely to have a significant adverse impact on the environment and are subject to a decision of a competent national authority.

Principle 18 States shall immediately notify other States of any natural disasters or other emergencies that are likely to produce sudden harmful effects on the environment of those States. Every effort shall be made by the international community to help States so affected.

The Rio Declaration

Principle 19 States shall provide prior and timely notification and relevant information to potentially affected States on activities that may have a significant adverse transboundary environmental effect and shall consult with those States at an early stage and in good faith.

Principle 20 Women have a vital role in environmental management and development. Their full participation is therefore essential to achieve sustainable development.

Principle 21 The creativity, ideals and courage of the youth of the world should be mobilized to forge a global partnership in order to achieve sustainable development and ensure a better future for all.

Principle 22 Indigenous people and their communities, and other local communities, have a vital role in environmental management and development because of their knowledge and traditional practices. States should recognize and duly support their identity, culture and interest and enable their effective participation in the achievement of sustainable development.

Principle 23 The environment and natural resources of people under oppression, domination and occupation shall be protected.

Principle 24 Warfare is inherently destructive of sustainable development. States shall therefore respect international law providing protection for the environment in times of armed conflict and cooperate in its further development, as necessary.

Principle 25 Peace, development and environmental protection are inter-dependent and indivisible.

Principle 26 States shall resolve all their environmental disputes peacefully and by appropriate means in accordance with the Charter of the United Nations.

Principle 27 States and people shall cooperate in good faith and in a spirit of partnership in the fulfilment of the principles embodied in this Declaration and in the further development of international law in the field of sustainable development.

Vienna Declaration and Programme of Action

The World Conference on Human Rights,

Considering that the promotion and protection of human rights is a matter of priority for the international community, and that the Conference affords a unique opportunity to carry out a comprehensive analysis of the international human rights system and of the machinery for the protection of human rights, in order to enhance and thus promote a fuller observance of those rights, in a just and balanced manner,

Recognizing and affirming that all human rights derive from the dignity and worth inherent in the human person, and that the human person is the central subject of human rights and fundamental freedoms, and consequently should be the principal beneficiary and should participate actively in the realization of these rights and freedoms,

Reaffirming their commitment to the purposes and principles contained in the Charter of the United Nations and the Universal Declaration of Human Rights,

Reaffirming the commitment contained in Article 56 of the Charter of the United Nations to take joint and separate action, placing proper emphasis on developing effective international cooperation for the realization of the purposes set out in Article 55, including universal respect for, and observance of, human rights and fundamental freedoms for all,

Emphasizing the responsibilities of all States, in conformity with the Charter of the United Nations, to develop and encourage respect for human rights and fundamental freedoms for all, without distinction as to race, sex, language or religion,

Recalling the Preamble to the Charter of the United Nations, in particular the determination to reaffirm faith in fundamental human rights, in the dignity and worth of the human person, and in the equal rights of men and women and of nations large and small,

Recalling also the determination expressed in the Preamble of the Charter of the United Nations to save succeeding generations from the scourge of war, to establish conditions under which justice and respect for obligations arising from treaties and other sources of international law can be maintained, to promote social progress and better standards of life in larger freedom, to practice tolerance and good neighbourliness, and to employ international machinery for the promotion of the economic and social advancement of all peoples,

Emphasizing that the Universal Declaration of Human Rights, which constitutes a common standard of achievement for all peoples and all nations, is the source of inspiration and has been the basis for the United Nations in making advances in standard setting as contained in the existing international human rights instruments, in particular the International Covenant on Civil and Political Rights and the International Covenant on Economic, Social and Cultural Rights,

Considering the major changes taking place on the international scene and the aspirations of all the peoples for an international order based on the principles enshrined in the Charter of the United Nations, including promoting and encouraging respect for human rights and fundamental freedoms for all the respect for the principle of equal rights and self-determination of peoples, peace, democracy, justice, equality, rule of law, pluralism, development, better standards of living and solidarity,

Deeply concerned by various forms of discrimination and violence, to which women continue to be exposed all over the world,

Recognizing that the activities of the United Nations in the field of human rights should be rationalized and enhanced in order to strengthen the United Nations machinery in this field and to further the objectives of universal respect for observance of international human rights standards,

Having taken into account the Declarations adopted by the three regional meetings at Tunis, San José and Bangkok and the contributions made by Governments, and bearing in mind the suggestions made by intergovernmental and non-governmental organizations, as well as the studies prepared by independent experts during the preparatory process leading to the World Conference on Human Rights,

Welcoming the International Year of the World's Indigenous Peoples 1993 as a reaffirmation of the commitment of the international community to ensure their enjoyment of all human rights and fundamental freedoms and to respect the value and diversity of their cultures and identities,

Recognizing also that the international community should devise ways and means to remove the current obstacles and meet challenges to the full realization of all human rights and to prevent the continuation of human rights violations resulting thereof throughout the world,

Invoking the spirit of our age and the realities of our time which call upon the peoples of the world and all States Members of the United Nations to rededicate themselves to the global task of promoting and protecting all human rights and fundamental freedoms so as to secure full and universal enjoyment of these rights,

Determined to take new steps forward in the commitment of the international community with a view to achieving substantial progress in human rights endeavours by an increased and sustained effort of international cooperation and solidarity,

Solemnly adopts the Vienna Declaration and Programme of Action.

I

1. The World Conference on Human Rights reaffirms the solemn commitment of all States to fulfil their obligations to promote universal respect for, and observance and protection of, all human rights and fundamental freedoms for all in accordance with the Charter of the United Nations, other instruments relating to human rights, and international law. The universal nature of these rights and freedoms is beyond question.

In this framework, enhancement of international cooperation in the field of human rights is essential for the full achievement of the purposes of the United Nations.

Human rights and fundamental freedoms are the birthright of all human beings; their protection and promotion is the first responsibility of Governments.

2. All peoples have the right of self-determination. By virtue of that right they freely determine their political status, and freely pursue their economic, social and cultural development.

Taking into account the particular situation of peoples under colonial or other forms of alien domination or foreign occupation, the World Conference on Human Rights recognizes the right of peoples to take any legitimate action, in accordance with the Charter of the United Nations, to realize their inalienable right of self-determination. The World Conference on Human Rights considers the denial of the right of self-determination as a violation of human rights and underlines the importance of the effective realization of this right.

In accordance with the Declaration on Principles of International Law concerning Friendly Relations and Cooperation Among States in accordance with the Charter of the United Nations, this shall not be construed as authorizing or encouraging any action which would dismember or impair, totally or in part, the territorial integrity or political unity of sovereign and independent States conducting themselves in compliance with the principle of equal rights and self-determination of peoples and thus possessed of a Government representing the whole people belonging to the territory without distinction of any kind.

3. Effective international measures to guarantee and monitor the implementation of human rights standards should be taken in respect of people under foreign occupation, and effective legal protection against the violation of their human rights should be provided, in accordance with human rights norms and international law, particularly the Geneva Convention relative to the Protection of Civilian Persons in Time of War, of 14 August 1949, and other applicable norms of humanitarian law.

4. The promotion and protection of all human rights and fundamental freedoms must be considered as a priority objective of the United Nations in accordance with its purposes and principles, in particular the purpose of international cooperation. In the framework of these purposes and principles, the promotion and protection of all human rights is a legitimate concern of the international community. The organs and specialized agencies related to human rights should therefore further enhance the coordination of their activities based on the consistent and objective application of international human rights instruments.

5. All human rights are universal, indivisible and interdependent and interrelated. The international community must treat human rights globally in a fair and equal manner, on the same footing, and with the same emphasis. While the significance of national and regional particularities and various historical, cultural and religious backgrounds must be borne in mind, it is the duty of States, regardless of their political, economic and cultural systems, to promote and protect all human rights and fundamental freedoms.

6. The efforts of the United Nations system towards the universal respect

for, and observance of, human rights and fundamental freedoms for all, contribute to the stability and well-being necessary for peaceful and friendly relations among nations, and to improved conditions for peace and security as well as social and economic development, in conformity with the Charter of the United Nations.

7. The processes of promoting and protecting human rights should be conducted in conformity with the purposes and principles of the Charter of the United Nations, and international law.

8. Democracy, development and respect for human rights and fundamental freedoms are interdependent and mutually reinforcing. Democracy is based on the freely expressed will of the people to determine their own political, economic, social and cultural systems and their full participation in all aspects of their lives. In the context of the above, the promotion and protection of human rights and fundamental freedoms at the national and international levels should be universal and conducted without conditions attached. The international community should support the strengthening and promoting of democracy, development and respect for human rights and fundamental freedoms in the entire world.

9. The World Conference on Human Rights reaffirms that least developed countries committed to the process of democratization and economic reforms, many of which are in Africa, should be supported by the international community in order to succeed in their transition to democracy and economic development.

10. The World Conference on Human Rights reaffirms the right to development, as established in the Declaration on the Right to Development, as a universal and inalienable right and an integral part of fundamental human rights.

As stated in the Declaration on the Right to Development, the human person is the central subject of development.

While development facilitates the enjoyment of all human rights, the lack of development may not be invoked to justify the abridgement of internationally recognized human rights.

States should cooperate with each other in ensuring development and eliminating obstacles to development. The international community should promote an effective international cooperation for the realization of the right to development and the elimination of obstacles to development.

Lasting progress towards the implementation of the right to development requires effective development policies at the national level, as well as equitable economic relations and a favourable economic environment at the international level.

11. The right to development should be fulfilled so as to meet equitably the developmental and environmental needs of present and future generations. The World Conference on Human Rights recognizes that illicit dumping of toxic and dangerous substances and waste potentially constitutes a serious threat to the human rights to life and health of everyone.

Consequently, the World Conference on Human Rights calls on all States to adopt and vigorously implement existing conventions relating to the dumping of toxic and dangerous products and waste and to cooperate in the prevention of illicit dumping.

Everyone has the right to enjoy the benefits of scientific progress and its applications. The World Conference on Human Rights notes that certain advances, notably in the biomedical and life sciences as well as in information technology, may have potentially adverse consequences for the integrity, dignity and human rights of the individual, and calls for international cooperation to ensure that human rights and dignity are fully respected in this area of universal concern.

12. The World Conference on Human Rights calls upon the international community to make all efforts to help alleviate the external debt burden of developing countries, in order to supplement the efforts of the Governments of such countries to attain the full realization of the economic, social and cultural rights of their people.

13. There is a need for States and international organizations, in cooperation with non-governmental organizations, to create favourable conditions at the national, regional and international levels to ensure the full and effective enjoyment of human rights. States should eliminate all violations of human rights and their causes, as well as obstacles to the enjoyment of these rights.

14. The existence of widespread extreme poverty inhibits the full and effective enjoyment of human rights; its immediate alleviation and eventual elimination must remain a high priority for the international community.

15. Respect for human rights and for fundamental freedoms without distinction of any kind is a fundamental rule of international human rights law. The speedy and comprehensive elimination of all forms of racism and racial discrimination, xenophobia and related intolerance is a priority task for the international community. Governments should take effective

measures to prevent and combat them. Groups, institutions, intergovernmental and non-governmental organizations and individuals are urged to intensify their efforts in cooperating and coordinating their activities against these evils.

16. The World Conference on Human Rights welcomes the progress made in dismantling apartheid and calls upon the international community and the United Nations system to assist in this process.

The World Conference on Human Rights also deplores the continuing acts of violence aimed at undermining the quest for a peaceful dismantling of apartheid.

17. The acts, methods and practices of terrorism in all its forms and manifestations as well as linkage in some countries to drug trafficking are activities aimed at the destruction of human rights, fundamental freedoms and democracy, threatening territorial integrity, security of States and destabilizing legitimately constituted Governments. The international community should take the necessary steps to enhance cooperation to prevent and combat terrorism.

18. The human rights of women and of the girl-child are an inalienable, integral and indivisible part of universal human rights. The full and equal participation of women in political, civil, economic, social and cultural life, at the national, regional and international levels, and the eradication of all forms of discrimination on grounds of sex are priority objectives of the international community.

Gender-based violence and all forms of sexual harassment and exploitation, including those resulting from cultural prejudice and international trafficking, are incompatible with the dignity and worth of the human person, and must be eliminated. This can be achieved by legal measures and through national action and international cooperation in such fields as economic and social development, education, safe maternity and health care, and social support.

The human rights of women should form an integral part of the United Nations human rights activities, including the promotion of all human rights instruments relating to women.

The World Conference on Human Rights urges Governments, institutions, intergovernmental and non-governmental organizations to intensify their efforts for the protection and promotion of human rights of women and the girl-child.

19. Considering the importance of the promotion and protection of the

rights of persons belonging to minorities and the contribution of such promotion and protection to the political and social stability of the States in which such persons live,

The World Conference on Human Rights reaffirms the obligation of States to ensure that persons belonging to minorities may exercise fully and effectively all human rights and fundamental freedoms without any discrimination and in full equality before the law in accordance with the Declaration on the Rights of Persons Belonging to National or Ethnic, Religious and Linguistic Minorities.

The persons belonging to minorities have the right to enjoy their own culture, to profess and practise their own religion and to use their own language in private and in public, freely and without interference or any form of discrimination.

20. The World Conference on Human Rights recognizes the inherent dignity and the unique contribution of indigenous people to the development and plurality of society and strongly reaffirms the commitment of the international community to their economic, social and cultural well-being and their enjoyment of the fruits of sustainable development. States should ensure the full and free participation of indigenous people in all aspects of society, in particular in matters of concern to them. Considering the importance of the promotion and protection of the rights of indigenous people, and the contribution of such promotion and protection to the political and social stability of the States in which such people live, States should, in accordance with international law, take concerted positive steps to ensure respect for all human rights and fundamental freedoms of indigenous people, on the basis of equality and non-discrimination, and recognize the value and diversity of their distinct identities, cultures and social organization.

21. The World Conference on Human Rights, welcoming the early ratification of the Convention on the Rights of the Child by a large number of States and noting the recognition of the human rights of children in the World Declaration on the Survival, Protection and Development of Children and Plan of Action adopted by the World Summit for Children, urges universal ratification of the Convention by 1995 and its effective implementation by States parties through the adoption of all the necessary legislative, administrative and other measures and the allocation to the maximum extent of the available resources. In all actions concerning children, non-discrimination and the best interest of the child should be

primary considerations and the views of the child given due weight. National and international mechanisms and programmes should be strengthened for the defence and protection of children, in particular, the girl-child, abandoned children, street children, economically and sexually exploited children, including through child pornography, child prostitution or sale of organs, children victims of diseases including acquired immuno-deficiency syndrome, refugee and displaced children, children in detention, children in armed conflict, as well as children victims of famine and drought and other emergencies. International cooperation and solidarity should be promoted to support the implementation of the Convention and the rights of the child should be a priority in the United Nations system-wide action on human rights.

The World Conference on Human Rights also stresses that the child for the full and harmonious development or his or her personality should grow up in a family environment which accordingly merits broader protection.

22. Special attention needs to be paid to ensuring non-discrimination, and the equal enjoyment of all human rights and fundamental freedoms by disabled persons, including their active participation in all aspects of society.

23. The World Conference on Human Rights reaffirms that everyone, without distinction of any kind, is entitled to the right to seek and to enjoy in other countries asylum from persecution, as well as the right to return to one's own country. In this respect it stresses the importance of the Universal Declaration of Human Rights, the 1951 Convention relating to the Status of Refugees, its 1967 Protocol and regional instruments. It expresses its appreciation to States that continue to admit and host large numbers of refugees in their territories, and to the Office of the United Nations High Commissioner for Refugees for its dedication to its task. It also expresses its appreciation to the United Nations Relief and Works Agency for Palestine Refugees in the Near East.

The World Conference on Human Rights recognizes that gross violations of human rights, including in armed conflicts, are among the multiple and complex factors leading to displacement of people.

The World Conference on Human Rights recognizes that, in view of the complexities of the global refugee crisis and in accordance with the Charter of the United Nations, relevant international instruments and international solidarity and in the spirit of burden-sharing, a comprehensive approach by the international community is needed in coordination and cooperation with the countries concerned and relevant organizations, bearing in mind the mandate of the United Nations High Commissioner for Refugees. This should include the development of strategies to address the root causes and effects of movements of refugees and other displaced persons, the strengthening of emergency preparedness and response mechanisms, the provision of effective protection and assistance, bearing in mind the special needs of women and children, as well as the achievement of durable solutions, primarily through the preferred solution of dignified and safe voluntary repatriation, including solutions such as those adopted by the international refugee conferences. The World Conference on Human Rights underlines the responsibilities of States, particularly as they relate to the countries of origin.

In the light of the comprehensive approach, the World Conference on Human Rights emphasizes the importance of giving special attention including through intergovernmental and humanitarian organizations and finding lasting solutions to questions related to internally displaced persons including their voluntary and safe return and rehabilitation.

In accordance with the Charter of the United Nations and the principles of humanitarian law, the World Conference on Human Rights further emphasizes the importance of and the need for humanitarian assistance to victims of all natural and man-made disasters.

24.   Great importance must be given to the promotion and protection of the human rights of persons belonging to groups which have been rendered vulnerable, including migrant workers, the elimination of all forms of discrimination against them, and the strengthening and more effective implementation of existing human rights instruments. States have an obligation to create and maintain adequate measures at the national level, in particular in the fields of education, health and social support for the promotion and protection of the rights of persons in vulnerable sectors of their populations and to ensure the participation of those among them who are interested in finding a solution to their own problems.

25.   The World Conference on Human Rights affirms that extreme poverty and social exclusion constitute a violation of human dignity and that urgent steps are necessary to achieve better knowledge of extreme poverty and its causes, including those related to the problem of development, in order to promote the human rights of the poorest, and to put an end to extreme poverty and social exclusion and to promote the enjoyment of the fruits of social progress. It is essential for States to foster participation

by the poorest people in the decision-making process by the community in which they live, the promotion of human rights and efforts to combat extreme poverty.

26. The World Conference on Human Rights welcomes the progress made in the codification of human rights instruments, which is a dynamic and evolving process, and urges the universal ratification of human rights treaties. All States are encouraged to accede to these international instruments; all States are encouraged to avoid, as far as possible, the resort to reservations.

27. Every State should provide an effective framework of remedies to redress human rights grievances or violations. The administration of justice, including law enforcement and prosecutorial agencies and, especially, an independent judiciary and legal profession in full conformity with applicable standards contained in international human rights instruments, are essential to the full and non-discriminatory realization of human rights and indispensable to the processes of democracy and sustainable development. In this context, institutions concerned with the administration of justice should be properly funded, and an increased level of both technical and financial assistance should be provided by the international community. It is incumbent upon the United Nations to make use of special programmes of advisory services on a priority basis for the achievement of a strong and independent administration of justice.

28. The World Conference on Human Rights expresses its dismay at massive violations of human rights especially in the form of genocide, 'ethnic cleansing' and systematic rape of women in war situations, creating mass exodus of refugees and displaced persons. While strongly condemning such abhorrent practices it reiterates the call that perpetrators of such crimes be punished and such practices immediately stopped.

29. The World Conference on Human Rights expresses grave concern about continuing human rights violations in all parts of the world in disregard of standards as contained in international human rights instruments and international humanitarian law and about the lack of sufficient and effective remedies for the victims.

The World Conference on Human Rights is deeply concerned about violations of human rights during armed conflicts, affecting the civilian population, especially women, children, the elderly and the disabled. The Conference therefore calls upon States and all parties to armed conflicts strictly to observe international humanitarian law, as set forth in the Geneva

Conventions of 1949 and other rules and principles of international law, as well as minimum standards for protection of human rights, as laid down in international conventions.

The World Conference on Human Rights reaffirms the right of the victims to be assisted by humanitarian organizations, as set forth in the Geneva Conventions of 1949 and other relevant instruments of international humanitarian law, and calls for the safe and timely access for such assistance.

30. The World Conference on Human Rights also expresses its dismay and condemnation that gross and systematic violations and situations that constitute serious obstacles to the full enjoyment of all human rights continue to occur in different parts of the world. Such violations and obstacles include, as well as torture and cruel, inhuman and degrading treatment or punishment, summary and arbitrary executions, disappearances, arbitrary detentions, all forms of racism, racial discrimination and apartheid, foreign occupation and alien domination, xenophobia, poverty, hunger and other denials of economic, social and cultural rights, religious intolerance, terrorism, discrimination against women and lack of the rule of law.

31. The World Conference on Human Rights calls upon States to refrain from any unilateral measure not in accordance with international law and the Charter of the United Nations that creates obstacles to trade relations among States and impedes the full realization of human rights set forth in the Universal Declaration of Human Rights and international human rights instruments, in particular the rights of everyone to a standard of living adequate for their health and well-being, including food and medical care, housing and the necessary social services. The World Conference on Human Rights affirms that food should not be used as a tool for political pressure.

32. The World Conference on Human Rights reaffirms the importance of ensuring the universality, objectivity and non-selectivity of the consideration of human rights issues.

33. The World Conference on Human Rights reaffirms that States are duty-bound, as stipulated in the Universal Declaration of Human Rights and the International Covenant on Economic, Social and Cultural Rights and in other international human rights instruments, to ensure that education is aimed at strengthening the respect of human rights and fundamental freedoms. The World Conference on Human Rights emphasizes the

importance of incorporating the subject of human rights education programmes and calls upon States to do so. Education should promote understanding, tolerance, peace and friendly relations between the nations and all racial or religious groups and encourage the development of United Nations activities in pursuance of these objectives. Therefore, education on human rights and the dissemination of proper information, both theoretical and practical, play an important role in the promotion and respect of human rights with regard to all individuals without distinction of any kind such as race, sex, language or religion, and this should be integrated in the education policies at the national as well as international levels. The World Conference on Human Rights notes that resource constraints and institutional inadequacies may impede the immediate realization of these objectives.

34. Increased efforts should be made to assist countries which so request to create the conditions whereby each individual can enjoy universal human rights and fundamental freedoms. Governments, the United Nations system as well as other multilateral organizations are urged to increase considerably the resources allocated to programmes aiming at the establishment and strengthening of national legislation, national institutions and related infrastructures which uphold the rule of law and democracy, electoral assistance, human rights awareness through training, teaching and education, popular participation and civil society.

The programmes of advisory services and technical cooperation under the Centre for Human Rights should be strengthened as well as made more efficient and transparent and thus become a major contribution to improving respect for human rights. States are called upon to increase their contributions to these programmes, both through promoting a larger allocation from the United Nations regular budget, and through voluntary contributions.

35. The full and effective implementation of United Nations activities to promote and protect human rights must reflect the high importance accorded to human rights by the Charter of the United Nations and the demands of the United Nations human rights activities, as mandated by Member States. To this end, United Nations human rights activities should be provided with increased resources.

36. The World Conference on Human Rights reaffirms the important and constructive role played by national institutions for the promotion and protection of human rights, in particular in their advisory capacity to the

competent authorities, their role in remedying human rights violations, in the dissemination of human rights information, and education in human rights.

The World Conference on Human Rights encourages the establishment and strengthening of national institutions, having regard to the 'Principles relating to the status of national institutions' and recognizing that it is the right of each State to choose the framework which is best suited to its particular needs at the national level.

37. Regional arrangements play a fundamental role in promoting and protecting human rights. They should reinforce universal human rights standards, as contained in international human rights instruments, and their protection. The World Conference on Human Rights endorses efforts under way to strengthen these arrangements and to increase their effectiveness, while at the same time stressing the importance of cooperation with the United Nations human rights activities.

The World Conference on Human Rights reiterates the need to consider the possibility of establishing regional and subregional arrangements for the promotion and protection of human rights where they do not already exist.

38. The World Conference on Human Rights recognizes the important role of non-governmental organizations in the promotion of all human rights and in humanitarian activities at national, regional and international levels. The World Conference on Human Rights appreciates their contribution to increasing public awareness of human rights issues, to the conduct of education, training and research in this field, and to the promotion and protection of all human rights and fundamental freedoms. While recognizing that the primary responsibility for standard-setting lies with States, the conference also appreciates the contribution of non-governmental organizations to this process. In this respect, the World Conference on Human Rights emphasizes the importance of continued dialogue and cooperation between Governments and non-governmental organizations. Non-governmental organizations and their members genuinely involved in the field of human rights should enjoy the rights and freedoms recognized in the Universal Declaration of Human Rights, and the protection of the national law. These rights and freedoms may not be exercised contrary to the purposes and principles of the United Nations. Non-governmental organizations should be free to carry out their human rights activities, without interference, within the framework of national law and the Universal Declaration of Human Rights.

39. Underlining the importance of objective, responsible and impartial information about human rights and humanitarian issues, the World Conference on Human Rights encourages the increased involvement of the media, for whom freedom and protection should be guaranteed within the framework of national law.

II

A. Increased coordination on human rights within the United Nations system

1. The World Conference on Human Rights recommends increased coordination in support of human rights and fundamental freedoms within the United Nations system. To this end, the World Conference on Human Rights urges all United Nations organs, bodies and the specialized agencies whose activities deal with human rights to cooperate in order to strengthen, rationalize and streamline their activities, taking into account the need to avoid unnecessary duplication. The World Conference on Human Rights also recommends to the Secretary-General that high-level officials of the relevant United Nations bodies and specialized agencies at their annual meeting, besides coordinating their activities, also assess the impact of their strategies and policies on the enjoyment of all human rights.

2. Furthermore, the World Conference on Human Rights calls on regional organizations and prominent international and regional finance and development institutions to assess also the impact of their policies and programmes on the enjoyment of human rights.

3. The World Conference on Human Rights recognizes that relevant specialized agencies and bodies and institutions of the United Nations system as well as other relevant intergovernmental organizations whose activities deal with human rights play a vital role in the formulation, promotion and implementation of human rights standards, within their respective mandates, and should take into account the outcome of the World Conference on Human Rights within their field of competence.

4. The World Conference on Human Rights strongly recommends that a concerted effort be made to encourage and facilitate the ratification of and accession or succession to international human rights treaties and protocols adopted within the framework of the United Nations system with the aim of universal acceptance. The Secretary-General, in consultation with treaty

bodies, should consider opening a dialogue with States not having acceded to these human rights treaties, in order to identify obstacles and to seek ways of overcoming them.

5. The World Conference on Human Rights encourages States to consider limiting the extent of any reservations they lodge to international human rights instruments, formulate any reservations as precisely and narrowly as possible, ensure that none is incompatible with the object and purpose of the relevant treaty and regularly review any reservations with a view to withdrawing them.

6. The World Conference on Human Rights, recognizing the need to maintain consistency with the high quality of existing international standards and to avoid proliferation of human rights instruments, reaffirms the guidelines relating to the elaboration of new international instruments contained in General Assembly resolution 41/120 of 4 December 1986 and calls on the United Nations human rights bodies, when considering the elaboration of new international standards, to keep those guidelines in mind, to consult with human rights treaty bodies on the necessity for drafting new standards and to request the Secretariat to carry out technical reviews of proposed new instruments.

7. The World Conference on Human Rights recommends that human rights officers be assigned if and when necessary to regional offices of the United Nations Organization with the purpose of disseminating information and offering training and other technical assistance in the field of human rights upon the request of concerned Member States. Human rights training for international civil servants who are assigned to work relating to human rights should be organized.

8. The World Conference on Human Rights welcomes the convening of emergency sessions of the Commission on Human Rights as a positive initiative and that other ways of responding to acute violations of human rights be considered by the relevant organs of the United Nations system.

Resources

9. The World Conference on Human Rights, concerned by the growing disparity between the activities of the Centre for Human Rights and the human, financial and other resources available to carry them out, and bearing in mind the resources needed for other important United Nations programmes, requests the Secretary-General and the General Assembly to take

Vienna Declaration

immediate steps to increase substantially the resources for the human rights programme from within the existing and future regular budgets of the United Nations, and to take urgent steps to seek increased extrabudgetary resources.

10. Within this framework, an increased proportion of the regular budget should be allocated directly to the Centre for Human Rights to cover its costs and all other costs borne by the Centre for Human Rights, including those related to the United Nations human rights bodies. Voluntary funding of the Centre's technical cooperation activities should reinforce this enhanced budget; the World Conference on Human Rights calls for generous contributions to the existing trust funds.

11. The World Conference on Human Rights requests the Secretary-General and the General Assembly to provide sufficient human, financial and other resources to the Centre for Human Rights to enable it effectively, efficiently and expeditiously to carry out its activities.

12. The World Conference on Human Rights, noting the need to ensure that human and financial resources are available to carry out the human rights activities, as mandated by intergovernmental bodies, urges the Secretary-General, in accordance with Article 101 of the Charter of the United Nations, and Member States to adopt a coherent approach aimed at securing that resources commensurate to the increased mandates are allocated to the Secretariat. The World Conference on Human Rights invites the Secretary-General to consider whether adjustments to procedures in the programme budget cycle would be necessary or helpful to ensure the timely and effective implementation of human rights activities as mandated by Member States.

Centre for Human Rights

13. The World Conference on Human Rights stresses the importance of strengthening the United Nations Centre for Human Rights.

14. The Centre for Human Rights should play an important role in coordinating system-wide attention for human rights. The focal role of the Centre can best be realized if it is enabled to cooperate fully with other United Nations bodies and organs. The coordinating role of the Centre for Human Rights also implies that the office of the Centre for Human Rights in New York is strengthened.

15. The Centre for Human Rights should be assured adequate means for the system of thematic and country rapporteurs, experts, working groups

and treaty bodies. Follow-up on recommendations should become a priority matter for consideration by the Commission on Human Rights.
16. The Centre for Human Rights should assume a larger role in the promotion of human rights. This role could be given shape through cooperation with Member States and by an enhanced programme of advisory services and technical assistance. The existing voluntary funds will have to be expanded substantially for these purposes and should be managed in a more efficient and coordinated way. All activities should follow strict and transparent project management rules and regular programme and project evaluations should be held periodically. To this end, the results of such evaluation exercises and other relevant information should be made available regularly. The Centre should, in particular, organize at least once a year information meetings open to all Member States and organizations directly involved in these projects and programmes.

Adaptation and strengthening of the United Nations machinery for human rights, including the question of the establishment of a United Nations High Commissioner for Human Rights

17. The World Conference on Human Rights recognizes the necessity for a continuing adaptation of the United Nations human rights machinery to the current and future needs in the promotion and protection of human rights, as reflected in the present Declaration and within the framework of a balanced and sustainable development for all people. In particular, the United Nations human rights organs should improve their coordination, efficiency and effectiveness.
18. The World Conference on Human Rights recommends to the General Assembly that when examining the report of the Conference at its forty-eighth session, it begin, as a matter of priority, consideration of the question of the establishment of a High Commissioner for Human Rights for the promotion and protection of all human rights.

B. Equality, dignity and tolerance

1. Racism, racial discrimination, xenophobia and other forms of intolerance

19. The World Conference on Human Rights considers the elimination of racism and racial discrimination, in particular in their institutionalized

forms such as apartheid or resulting from doctrines of racial superiority or exclusivity or contemporary forms and manifestations of racism, as a primary objective for the international community and a worldwide promotion programme in the field of human rights. United Nations organs and agencies should strengthen their efforts to implement such a programme of action related to the third decade to combat racism and racial discrimination as well as subsequent mandates to the same end. The World Conference on Human Rights strongly appeals to the international community to contribute generously to the Trust Fund for the Programme for the Decade for Action to Combat Racism and Racial Discrimination.

20. The World Conference on Human Rights urges all Governments to take immediate measures and to develop strong policies to prevent and combat all forms and manifestations of racism, xenophobia or related intolerance, where necessary by enactment of appropriate legislation, including penal measures, and by the establishment of national institutions to combat such phenomena.

21. The World Conference on Human Rights welcomes the decision of the Commission on Human Rights to appoint a Special Rapporteur on contemporary forms of racism, racial discrimination, xenophobia and related intolerance. The World Conference on Human Rights also appeals to all States parties to the International Convention on the Elimination of All Forms of Racial Discrimination to consider making the declaration under article 14 of the Convention.

22. The World Conference on Human Rights calls upon all Governments to take all appropriate measures in compliance with their international obligations and with due regard to their respective legal systems to counter intolerance and related violence based on religion or belief, including practices of discrimination against women and including the desecration of religious sites, recognizing that every individual has the right to freedom of thought, conscience, expression and religion. The Conference also invites all States to put into practice the provisions of the Declaration on the Elimination of All Forms of Intolerance and of Discrimination Based on Religion or Belief.

23. The World Conference on Human Rights stresses that all persons who perpetrate or authorize criminal acts associated with ethnic cleansing are individually responsible and accountable for such human rights violations, and that the international community should exert every effort to bring those legally responsible for such violations to justice.

24.   The World Conference on Human Rights calls on all States to take immediate measures, individually and collectively, to combat the practice of ethnic cleansing to bring it quickly to an end. Victims of the abhorrent practice of ethnic cleansing are entitled to appropriate and effective remedies.

2. Persons belonging to national or ethnic, religious and linguistic minorities

25.   The World Conference on Human Rights calls on the Commission on Human Rights to examine ways and means to promote and protect effectively the rights of persons belonging to minorities as set out in the Declaration on the Rights of Persons belonging to National or Ethnic, Religious and Linguistic Minorities. In this context, the World Conference on Human Rights calls upon the Centre for Human Rights to provide, at the request of Governments concerned and as part of its programme of advisory services and technical assistance, qualified expertise on minority issues and human rights, as well as on the prevention and resolution of disputes, to assist in existing or potential situations involving minorities.
26.   The World Conference on Human Rights urges States and the international community to promote and protect the rights of persons belonging to national or ethnic, religious and linguistic minorities in accordance with the Declaration on the Rights of Persons belonging to National or Ethnic, Religious and Linguistic Minorities.
27.   Measures to be taken, where appropriate, should include facilitation of their full participation in all aspects of the political, economic, social, religious and cultural life of society and in the economic progress and development in their country.

Indigenous people

28.   The World Conference on Human Rights calls on the Working Group on Indigenous Populations of the Sub-Commission on Prevention of Discrimination and Protection of Minorities to complete the drafting of a declaration on the rights of indigenous people at its eleventh session.
29.   The World Conference on Human Rights recommends that the Commission on Human Rights consider the renewal and updating of the mandate of the Working Group on Indigenous Populations upon completion of the drafting of a declaration on the rights of indigenous peoples.

30. The World Conference on Human Rights also recommends that advisory services and technical assistance programmes within the United Nations system respond positively to requests by States for assistance which would be of direct benefit to indigenous people. The World Conference on Human Rights further recommends that adequate human and financial resources be made available to the Centre for Human Rights within the overall framework of strengthening the Centre's activities as envisaged by this document.

31. The World Conference on Human Rights urges States to ensure the full and free participation of indigenous people in all aspects of society, in particular in matters of concern to them.

32. The World Conference on Human Rights recommends that the General Assembly proclaim an international decade of the world's indigenous people, to begin from January 1994, including action-orientated programmes, to be decided upon in partnership with indigenous people. An appropriate voluntary trust fund should be set up for this purpose. In the framework of such a decade, the establishment of a permanent forum for indigenous people in the United Nations system should be considered.

Migrant workers

33. The World Conference on Human Rights urges all States to guarantee the protection of the human rights of all migrant workers and their families.

34. The World Conference on Human Rights considers that the creation of conditions to foster greater harmony and tolerance between migrant workers and the rest of the society of the State in which they reside is of particular importance.

35. The World Conference on Human Rights invites States to consider the possibility of signing and ratifying, at the earliest possible time, the International Convention on the Rights of All Migrant Workers and Members of Their Families.

3. The equal status and human rights of women

36. The World Conference on Human Rights urges the full and equal enjoyment by women of all human rights and that this be a priority for Governments and for the United Nations. The World Conference on

Human Rights also underlines the importance of the integration and full participation of women as both agents and beneficiaries of the development process, and reiterates the objectives established on global action for women towards sustainable and equitable development set forth in the Rio Declaration on Environment and Development and chapter 24 of Agenda 21, adopted by the United Nations Conference on Environment and Development (Rio de Janeiro, Brazil, 3–14 June 1992).

37. The equal status of women and the human rights of women should be integrated into the mainstream of United Nations system-wide activity. These issues should be regularly and systematically addressed throughout relevant United Nations bodies and mechanisms. In particular, steps should be taken to increase cooperation and promote further integration of objectives and goals between the Commission on the Status of Women, the Commission on Human Rights, the Committee for the Elimination of Discrimination against Women, the United Nations Development Fund for Women, the United Nations Development Programme and other United Nations agencies. In this context, cooperation and coordination should be strengthened between the Centre for Human Rights and the Division for the Advancement of Women.

38. In particular, the World Conference on Human Rights stresses the importance of working towards the elimination of violence against women in public and private life, the elimination of all forms of sexual harassment, exploitation and trafficking in women, the elimination of gender bias in the administration of justice and the eradication of any conflicts which may arise between the rights of women and the harmful effects of certain traditional or customary practices, cultural prejudices and religious extremism. The World Conference on Human Rights calls upon the General Assembly to adopt the draft declaration on violence against women and urges States to combat violence against women in accordance with its provisions. Violations of the human rights of women in situations of armed conflict are violations of the fundamental principles of international human rights and humanitarian law. All violations of this kind, including in particular murder, systematic rape, sexual slavery, and forced pregnancy, require a particularly effective response.

39. The World Conference on Human Rights urges the eradication of all forms of discrimination against women, both hidden and overt. The United Nations should encourage the goal of universal ratification by all States of the Convention on the Elimination of All Forms of Discrimination against

Women by the year 2000. Ways and means of addressing the particularly large number of reservations to the Convention should be encouraged. *Inter alia*, the Committee on the Elimination of Discrimination against Women should continue its review of reservations to the Convention. States are urged to withdraw reservations that are contrary to the object and purpose of the Convention or which are otherwise incompatible with international treaty law.

40. Treaty monitoring bodies should disseminate necessary information to enable women to make more effective use of existing implementation procedures in their pursuits of full and equal enjoyment of human rights and non-discrimination. New procedures should also be adopted to strengthen implementation of the commitment to women's equality and the human rights of women. The Commission on the Status of Women and the Committee on the Elimination of Discrimination against Women should quickly examine the possibility of introducing the right of petition through the preparation of an optional protocol to the Convention on the Elimination of All Forms of Discrimination against Women. The World Conference on Human Rights welcomes the decision of the Commission on Human Rights to consider the appointment of a special rapporteur on violence against women at its fiftieth session.

41. The World Conference on Human Rights recognizes the importance of the enjoyment by women of the highest standard of physical and mental health throughout their life span. In the context of the World Conference on Women and the Convention on the Elimination of All Forms of Discrimination against Women, as well as the Proclamation of Tehran of 1968, the World Conference on Human Rights reaffirms, on the basis of equality between women and men, a woman's right to accessible and adequate health care and the widest range of family planning services, as well as equal access to education at all levels.

42. Treaty monitoring bodies should include the status of women and the human rights of women in their deliberations and findings, making use of gender-specific data. States should be encouraged to supply information on the situation of women *de jure* and *de facto* in their reports to treaty monitoring bodies. The World Conference on Human Rights notes with satisfaction that the Commission on Human Rights adopted at its forty-ninth session resolution 1993/46 of 8 March 1993 stating that rapporteurs and working groups in the field of human rights should also be encouraged to do so. Steps should also be taken by the Division for the Advancement of

Women in cooperation with other United Nations bodies, specifically the Centre for Human Rights, to ensure that the human rights activities of the United Nations regularly address violations of women's human rights, including gender-specific abuses. Training for United Nations human rights and humanitarian relief personnel to assist them to recognize and deal with human rights abuses particular to women and to carry out their work without gender bias should be encouraged.

43. The World Conference on Human Rights urges Governments and regional and international organizations to facilitate the access of women to decision-making posts and their greater participation in the decision-making process. It encourages further steps within the United Nations Secretariat to appoint and promote women staff members in accordance with the Charter of the United Nations, and encourages other principal and subsidiary organs of the United Nations to guarantee the participation of women under conditions of equality.

44. The World Conference on Human Rights welcomes the World Conference on Women to be held in Beijing in 1995 and urges that human rights of women should play an important role in its deliberations, in accordance with the priority themes of the World Conference on Women of equality, development and peace.

4. The rights of the child

45. The World Conference on Human Rights reiterates the principle of 'First Call for Children' and, in this respect, underlines the importance of major national and international efforts, especially those of the United Nations Children's Fund, for promoting respect for the rights of the child to survival, protection, development and participation.

46. Measures should be taken to achieve universal ratification of the Convention on the Rights of the Child by 1995 and the universal signing of the World Declaration on the Survival, Protection and Development of Children and Plan of Action adopted by the World Summit for Children, as well as their effective implementation. The World Conference on Human Rights urges States to withdraw reservations to the Convention on the Rights of the Child contrary to the object and purpose of the Convention or otherwise contrary to international treaty law.

47. The World Conference on Human Rights urges all nations to undertake measures to the maximum extent of their available resources, with the

support of international cooperation, to achieve the goals in the World Summit Plan of Action. The Conference calls on States to integrate the Convention on the Rights of the Child into their national action plans. By means of these national action plans and through international efforts, particular priority should be placed on reducing infant and maternal mortality rates, reducing malnutrition and illiteracy rates and providing access to safe drinking water and to basic education. Whenever so called for, national plans of action should be devised to combat devastating emergencies resulting from natural disasters and armed conflicts and the equally grave problem of children in extreme poverty.

48. The World Conference on Human Rights urges all States, with the support of international cooperation, to address the acute problem of children under especially difficult circumstances. Exploitation and abuse of children should be actively combated, including by addressing their root causes. Effective measures are required against female infanticide, harmful child labour, sale of children and organs, child prostitution, child pornography, as well as other forms of sexual abuse.

49. The World Conference on Human Rights supports all measures by the United Nations and its specialized agencies to ensure the effective protection and promotion of human rights of the girl-child. The World Conference on Human Rights urges States to repeal existing laws and regulations and remove customs and practices which discriminate against and cause harm to the girl-child.

50. The World Conference on Human Rights strongly supports the proposal that the Secretary-General initiate a study into means of improving the protection of children in armed conflicts. Humanitarian norms should be implemented and measures taken in order to protect and facilitate assistance to children in war zones. Measures should include protection for children against indiscriminate use of all weapons of war, especially anti-personnel mines. The need for aftercare and rehabilitation of children traumatized by war must be addressed urgently. The Conference calls on the Committee on the Rights of the Child to study the question of raising the minimum age of recruitment into armed forces.

51. The World Conference on Human Rights recommends that matters relating to human rights and the situation of children be regularly reviewed and monitored by all relevant organs and mechanisms of the United Nations system and by the supervisory bodies of the specialized agencies in accordance with their mandates.

52. The World Conference on Human Rights recognizes the important role played by non-governmental organizations in the effective implementation of all human rights instruments and, in particular, the Convention on the Rights of the Child.

53. The World Conference on Human Rights recommends that the Committee on the Rights of the Child, with the assistance of the Centre for Human Rights, be enabled expeditiously and effectively to meet its mandate, especially in view of the unprecedented extent of ratification and subsequent submission of country reports.

5. Freedom from torture

54. The World Conference on Human Rights welcomes the ratification by many Member States of the Convention against Torture and Other Cruel, Inhuman or Degrading Treatment or Punishment and encourages its speedy ratification by all other Member States.

55. The World Conference on Human Rights emphasizes that one of the most atrocious violations against human dignity is the act of torture, the result of which destroys the dignity and impairs the capability of victims to continue their lives and their activities.

56. The World Conference on Human Rights reaffirms that under human rights law and international humanitarian law, freedom from torture is a right which must be protected under all circumstances, including in times of internal or international disturbance or armed conflicts.

57. The World Conference on Human Rights therefore urges all States to put an immediate end to the practice of torture and eradicate this evil forever through full implementation of the Universal Declaration of Human Rights as well as the relevant conventions and, where necessary, strengthening of existing mechanisms. The World Conference on Human Rights calls on all States to cooperate fully with the Special Rapporteur on the question of torture in the fulfilment of his mandate.

58. Special attention should be given to ensure universal respect for, and effective implementation of, the Principles of Medical Ethics relevant to the Role of Health Personnel, particularly Physicians, in the Protection of Prisoners and Detainees against Torture and other Cruel, Inhuman or Degrading Treatment or Punishment adopted by the General Assembly of the United Nations.

59. The World Conference on Human Rights stresses the importance of further concrete action within the framework of the United Nations with the view to providing assistance to victims of torture and ensure more effective remedies for their physical, psychological and social rehabilitation. Providing the necessary resources for this purpose should be given high priority, *inter alia*, by additional contributions to the United Nations Voluntary Fund for the Victims of Torture.

60. States should abrogate legislation leading to impunity for those responsible for grave violations of human rights such as torture and prosecute such violations, thereby providing a firm basis for the rule of law.

61. The World Conference on Human Rights reaffirms that efforts to eradicate torture should, first and foremost, be concentrated on prevention and, therefore, calls for the early adoption of an optional protocol to the Convention against Torture and Other Cruel, Inhuman and Degrading Treatment or Punishment, which is intended to establish a preventive system of regular visits to places of detention.

Enforced disappearances

62. The World Conference on Human Rights, welcoming the adoption by the General Assembly of the Declaration on the Protection of All Persons from Enforced Disappearance, calls upon all States to take effective legislative, administrative, judicial or other measures to prevent, terminate and punish acts of enforced disappearances. The World Conference on Human Rights reaffirms that it is the duty of all States, under any circumstances, to make investigations whenever there is reason to believe that an enforced disappearance has taken place on a territory under their jurisdiction and, if allegations are confirmed, to prosecute its perpetrators.

6. The rights of the disabled person

63. The World Conference on Human Rights reaffirms that all human rights and fundamental freedoms are universal and thus unreservedly include persons with disabilities. Every person is born equal and has the same rights to life and welfare, education and work, living independently and active participation in all aspects of society. Any direct discrimination or other negative discriminatory treatment of a disabled person is therefore

a violation of his or her rights. The World Conference on Human Rights calls on Governments, where necessary, to adopt or adjust legislation to assure access to these and other rights for disabled persons.

64. The place of disabled persons is everywhere. Persons with disabilities should be guaranteed equal opportunity through the elimination of all socially determined barriers, be they physical, financial, social or psychological, which exclude or restrict full participation in society.

65. Recalling the World Programme of Action concerning Disabled Persons, adopted by the General Assembly at its thirty-seventh session, the World Conference on Human Rights calls upon the General Assembly and the Economic and Social Council to adopt the draft standard rules on the equalization of opportunities for persons with disabilities, at their meetings in 1993.

C. Cooperation, development and strengthening of human rights

66. The World Conference on Human Rights recommends that priority be given to national and international action to promote democracy, development and human rights.

67. Special emphasis should be given to measures to assist in the strengthening and building of institutions relating to human rights, strengthening of a pluralistic civil society and the protection of groups which have been rendered vulnerable. In this context, assistance provided upon the request of Governments for the conduct of free and fair elections, including assistance in the human rights aspects of elections and public information about elections, is of particular importance. Equally important is the assistance to be given to the strengthening of the rule of law, the promotion of freedom of expression and the administration of justice, and to the real and effective participation of the people in the decision-making processes.

68. The World Conference on Human Rights stresses the need for the implementation of strengthened advisory services and technical assistance activities by the Centre for Human Rights. The Centre should make available to States upon request assistance on specific human rights issues, including the preparation of reports under human rights treaties as well as for the implementation of coherent and comprehensive plans of action for the promotion and protection of human rights. Strengthening the institutions of human rights and democracy, the legal protection of human rights, training of officials and others, broad-based education and public information aimed at promoting respect for human rights should all be available as components of these programmes.

69.   The World Conference on Human Rights strongly recommends that a comprehensive programme be established within the United Nations in order to help States in the task of building and strengthening adequate national structures which have a direct impact on the overall observance of human rights and the maintenance of the rule of law. Such a programme, to be coordinated by the Centre for Human Rights, should be able to provide, upon the request of the interested Government, technical and financial assistance to national projects in reforming penal and correctional establishments, education and training of lawyers, judges and security forces in human rights, and any other sphere of activity relevant to the good functioning of the rule of law. That programme should make available to States assistance for the implementation of plans of action for the promotion and protection of human rights.

70.   The World Conference on Human Rights requests the Secretary-General of the United Nations to submit proposals to the United Nations General Assembly, containing alternatives for the establishment, structure, operational modalities and funding of the proposed programme.

71.   The World Conference on Human Rights recommends that each State consider the desirability of drawing up a national action plan identifying steps whereby that State would improve the promotion and protection of human rights.

72.   The World Conference on Human Rights reaffirms that the universal and inalienable right to development, as established in the Declaration on the Right to Development, must be implemented and realized. In this context, the World Conference on Human Rights welcomes the appointment by the Commission on Human Rights of a thematic working group on the right to development and urges that the Working Group, in consultation and cooperation with other organs and agencies of the United Nations system, promptly formulate, for early consideration by the United Nations General Assembly, comprehensive and effective measures to eliminate obstacles to the implementation and realization of the Declaration on the Right to Development and recommending ways and means towards the realization of the right to development by all States.

73. The World Conference on Human Rights recommends that non-governmental and other grass-roots organizations active in development and/or human rights should be enabled to play a major role on the national and international levels in the debate, activities and implementation relating to the right to development and, in cooperation with Governments, in all relevant aspects of development cooperation.

74. The World Conference on Human Rights appeals to Governments, competent agencies and institutions to increase considerably the resources devoted to building well-functioning legal systems able to protect human rights, and to national institutions working in this area. Actors in the field of development cooperation should bear in mind the mutually reinforcing interrelationship between development, democracy and human rights. Cooperation should be based on dialogue and transparency. The World Conference on Human Rights also calls for the establishment of comprehensive programmes, including resource banks of information and personnel with expertise relating to the strengthening of the rule of law and of democratic institutions.

75. The World Conference on Human Rights encourages the Commission on Human Rights, in cooperation with the Committee on Economic, Social and Cultural Rights, to continue the examination of optional protocols to the International Covenant on Economic, Social and Cultural Rights.

76. The World Conference on Human Rights recommends that more resources be made available for the strengthening or the establishment of regional arrangements for the promotion and protection of human rights under the programmes of advisory services and technical assistance of the Centre for Human Rights. States are encouraged to request assistance for such purposes as regional and subregional workshops, seminars and information exchanges designed to strengthen regional arrangements for the promotion and protection of human rights in accord with universal human rights standards as contained in international human rights instruments.

77. The World Conference on Human Rights supports all measures by the United Nations and its relevant specialized agencies to ensure the effective promotion and protection of trade union rights, as stipulated in the International Covenant on Economic, Social and Cultural Rights and other relevant international instruments. It calls on all States to abide fully by their obligations in this regard contained in international instruments.

D. Human rights education

78.   The World Conference on Human Rights considers human rights education, training and public information essential for the promotion and achievement of stable and harmonious relations among communities and for fostering mutual understanding, tolerance and peace.

79.   States should strive to eradicate illiteracy and should direct education towards the full development of the human personality and to the strengthening of respect for human rights and fundamental freedoms. The World Conference on Human Rights calls on all States and institutions to include human rights, humanitarian law, democracy and rule of law as subjects in the curricula of all learning institutions in formal and non-formal settings.

80.   Human rights education should include peace, democracy, development and social justice, as set forth in international and regional human rights instruments, in order to achieve common understanding and awareness with a view to strengthening universal commitment to human rights.

81.   Taking into account the World Plan of Action on Education for Human Rights and Democracy, adopted in March 1993 by the International Congress on Education for Human Rights and Democracy of the United Nations Educational, Scientific and Cultural Organization, and other human rights instruments, the World Conference on Human Rights recommends that States develop specific programmes and strategies for ensuring the widest human rights education and the dissemination of public information, taking particular account of the human rights needs of women.

82.   Governments, with the assistance of intergovernmental organizations, national institutions and non-governmental organizations, should promote an increased awareness of human rights and mutual tolerance. The World Conference on Human Rights underlines the importance of strengthening the World Public Information Campaign for Human Rights carried out by the United Nations. They should initiate and support education in human rights and undertake effective dissemination of public information in this field. The advisory services and technical assistance programmes of the United Nations system should be able to respond immediately to requests from States for educational and training activities in the field of human rights as well as for special education concerning standards as contained in international human rights instruments and in humanitarian law and their

application to special groups such as military forces, law enforcement personnel, police and the health profession. The proclamation of a United Nations decade for human rights education in order to promote, encourage and focus these educational activities should be considered.

E. Implementation and monitoring methods

83. The World Conference on Human Rights urges Governments to incorporate standards as contained in international human rights instruments in domestic legislation and to strengthen national structures, institutions and organs of society which play a role in promoting and safeguarding human rights.

84. The World Conference on Human Rights recommends the strengthening of United Nations activities and programmes to meet requests for assistance by States which want to establish or strengthen their own national institutions for the promotion and protection of human rights.

85. The World Conference on Human Rights also encourages the strengthening of cooperation between national institutions for the promotion and protection of human rights, particularly through exchanges of information and experience, as well as cooperation with regional organizations and the United Nations.

86. The World Conference on Human Rights strongly recommends in this regard that representatives of national institutions for the promotion and protection of human rights convene periodic meetings under the auspices of the Centre for Human Rights to examine ways and means of improving their mechanisms and sharing experiences.

87. The World Conference on Human Rights recommends to the human rights treaty bodies, to the meetings of chairpersons of the treaty bodies and to the meetings of States parties that they continue to take steps aimed at coordinating the multiple reporting requirements and guidelines for preparing State reports under the respective human rights conventions and study the suggestion that the submission of one overall report on treaty obligations undertaken by each State would make these procedures more effective and increase their impact.

88. The World Conference on Human Rights recommends that the States parties to international human rights instruments, the General Assembly and the Economic and Social Council should consider studying

the existing human rights treaty bodies and the various thematic mechanisms and procedures with a view to promoting greater efficiency and effectiveness through better coordination of the various bodies, mechanisms and procedures, taking into account the need to avoid unnecessary duplication and overlapping of their mandates and tasks.

89. The World Conference on Human Rights recommends continued work on the improvement of the functioning, including the monitoring tasks, of the treaty bodies, taking into account multiple proposals made in this respect, in particular those made by the treaty bodies themselves and by the meetings of the chairpersons of the treaty bodies. The comprehensive national approach taken by the Committee on the Rights of the Child should also be encouraged.

90. The World Conference on Human Rights recommends that States parties to human rights treaties consider accepting all the available optional communication procedures.

91. The World Conference on Human Rights views with concern the issue of impunity of perpetrators of human rights violations, and supports the efforts of the Commission on Human Rights and the Sub-Commission on Prevention of Discrimination and Protection of Minorities to examine all aspects of the issue.

92. The World Conference on Human Rights recommends that the Commission on Human Rights examine the possibility for better implementation of existing human rights instruments at the international and regional levels and encourages the International Law Commission to continue its work on an international criminal court.

93. The World Conference on Human Rights appeals to States which have not yet done so to accede to the Geneva Conventions of 12 August 1949 and the Protocols thereto, and to take all appropriate national measures, including legislative ones, for their full implementation.

94. The World Conference on Human Rights recommends the speedy completion and adoption of the draft declaration on the right and responsibility of individuals, groups and organs of society to promote and protect universally recognized human rights and fundamental freedoms.

95. The World Conference on Human Rights underlines the importance of preserving and strengthening the system of special procedures, rapporteurs, representatives, experts and working groups of the Commission on Human Rights and the Sub-Commission on the Prevention of Discrimination and Protection of Minorities, in order to enable them to

carry out their mandates in all countries throughout the world, providing them with the necessary human and financial resources. The procedures and mechanisms should be enabled to harmonize and rationalize their work through periodic meetings. All States are asked to cooperate fully with these procedures and mechanisms.

96. The World Conference on Human Rights recommends that the United Nations assume a more active role in the promotion and protection of human rights in ensuring full respect for international humanitarian law in all situations of armed conflict, in accordance with the purposes and principles of the Charter of the United Nations.

97. The World Conference on Human Rights, recognizing the important role of human rights components in specific arrangements concerning some peace-keeping operations by the United Nations, recommends that the Secretary-General take into account the reporting, experience and capabilities of the Centre for Human Rights and human rights mechanisms, in conformity with the Charter of the United Nations.

98. To strengthen the enjoyment of economic, social and cultural rights, additional approaches should be examined, such as a system of indicators to measure progress in the realization of the rights set forth in the International Covenant on Economic, Social and Cultural Rights. There must be a concerted effort to ensure recognition of economic, social and cultural rights at the national, regional and international levels.

F. Follow-up to the World Conference on Human Rights

99. The World Conference on Human Rights recommends that the General Assembly, the Commission on Human Rights and other organs and agencies of the United Nations system related to human rights consider ways and means for the full implementation, without delay, of the recommendations contained in the present Declaration, including the possibility of proclaiming a United Nations decade for human rights. The World Conference on Human Rights further recommends that the Commission on Human Rights annually review the progress towards this end.

100. The World Conference on Human Rights requests the Secretary-General of the United Nations to invite on the occasion of the fiftieth anniversary of the Universal Declaration of Human Rights all States, all organs and agencies of the United Nations system related to human rights, to report to him on the progress made in the implementation of the present

Declaration and to submit a report to the General Assembly at its fifty-third session, through the Commission on Human Rights and the Economic and Social Council. Likewise, regional and, as appropriate, national human rights institutions, as well as non-governmental organizations, may present their views to the Secretary-General on the progress made in the implementation of the present Declaration. Special attention should be paid to assessing the progress towards the goal of universal ratification of international human rights treaties and protocols adopted within the framework of the United Nations system.

A Global Ethic

The Declaration of a Global Ethic

The world is in agony. The agony is so pervasive and urgent that we are compelled to name its manifestations so that the depth of this pain may be made clear.

Peace eludes us . . . the planet is being destroyed . . . neighbors live in fear . . . women and men are estranged from each other . . . children die!

This is abhorrent!

We condemn the abuses of Earth's ecosystems.

We condemn the poverty that stifles life's potential; the hunger that weakens the human body; the economic disparities that threaten so many families with ruin.

We condemn the social disarray of the nations; the disregard for justice which pushes citizens to the margin; the anarchy overtaking our communities; and the insane death of children from violence. In particular we condemn aggression and hatred in the name of religion.

But this agony need not be.

It need not be because the basis for an ethic already exists. This ethic offers the possibility of a better individual and global order, and leads individuals away from despair and societies away from chaos.

We are women and men who have embraced the precepts and practices of the world's religions:

We affirm that a common set of core values is found in the teachings of the religions, and that these form the basis of a global ethic.

We affirm that this truth is already known, but yet to be lived in heart and action.

We affirm that there is an irrevocable, unconditional norm for all areas of life, for families and communities, for races, nations, and religions. There already exist ancient guidelines for human behavior which are found in the teachings of the religions of the world and which are the condition for a sustainable world order.

We Declare:

We are interdependent. Each of us depends on the well-being of the whole, and so we have respect for the community of living beings, for people, animals, and plants, and for the preservation of Earth, the air, water and soil.

We take individual responsibility for all we do. All our decisions, actions, and failures to act have consequences.

We must treat others as we wish others to treat us. We make a commitment to respect life and dignity, individuality and diversity, so that every person is treated humanely, without exception. We must have patience and acceptance. We must be able to forgive, learning from the past but never allowing ourselves to be enslaved by memories of hate. Opening our hearts to one another, we must sink our narrow differences for the cause of the world community, practicing a culture of solidarity and relatedness.

We consider humankind our family. We must strive to be kind and generous. We must not live for ourselves alone, but should also serve others, never forgetting the children, the aged, the poor, the suffering, the disabled, the refugees, and the lonely. No person should ever be considered or treated as a second-class citizen, or be exploited in any way whatsoever. There should be equal partnership between men and women. We must not commit any kind of sexual immorality. We must put behind us all forms of domination or abuse.

We commit ourselves to a culture of non-violence, respect, justice, and peace. We shall not oppress, injure, torture, or kill other human beings, forsaking violence as a means of settling differences.

We must strive for a just social and economic order, in which everyone has an equal chance to reach full potential as a human being. We must speak and act truthfully and with compassion, dealing fairly with all, and avoiding prejudice and hatred. We must not steal. We must move beyond the dominance of greed for power, prestige, money, and consumption to make a just and peaceful world.

Earth cannot be changed for the better unless the consciousness of individuals is changed first. We pledge to increase our awareness by disciplining our minds, by meditation, by prayer, or by positive thinking. Without risk and a readiness to sacrifice there can be no fundamental change in our situation. Therefore we commit ourselves to this global ethic, to understanding one another, and to socially beneficial, peace-fostering, and nature-friendly ways of life.

We invite all people, whether religious or not, to do the same.

The Principles of a Global Ethic

Our world is experiencing a fundamental crisis: A crisis in global economy, global ecology, and global politics. The lack of a grand vision, the tangle of unresolved problems, political paralysis, mediocre political leadership with little insight or foresight, and in general too little sense for the commonweal are seen everywhere: Too many old answers to new challenges.

Hundreds of millions of human beings on our planet increasingly suffer from unemployment, poverty, hunger, and the destruction of their families. Hope for a lasting peace among nations slips away from us. There are tensions between the sexes and generations. Children die, kill, and are killed. More and more countries are shaken by corruption in politics and business. It is increasingly difficult to live together peacefully in our cities because of social, racial, and ethnic conflicts, the abuse of drugs, organized crime, and even anarchy. Even neighbors often live in fear of one another. Our planet continues to be ruthlessly plundered. A collapse of the ecosystem threatens us.

Time and again we see leaders and members of religions incite aggression, fanaticism, hate, and xenophobia – even inspire and legitimize violent and bloody conflicts. Religion often is misused for purely power-political goals, including war. We are filled with disgust.

We condemn these blights and declare that they need not be. An ethic already exists within the religious teachings of the world which can counter the global distress. Of course this ethic provides no direct solution for all the immense problems of the world, but it does supply the moral foundation for a better individual and global order: A vision which can lead women and men away from despair, and society away from chaos.

We are persons who have committed ourselves to the precepts and practices of the world's religions. We confirm that there is already a consensus among the religions which can be the basis for a global ethic – a minimal *fundamental consensus* concerning binding *values,* irrevocable *standards,* and *fundamental moral attitudes.*

I. No new global order without a new global ethic!

We women and men of various religions and regions of Earth therefore address all people, religious and non-religious. We wish to express the following convictions which we hold in common:

- We all have a responsibility for a better global order.
- Our involvement for the sake of human rights, freedom, justice, peace and the preservation of Earth is absolutely necessary.
- Our different religious and cultural traditions must not prevent our common involvement in opposing all forms of inhumanity and working for greater humaneness.
- The principles expressed in this Global Ethic can be affirmed by all persons with ethical convictions, whether religiously grounded or not.
- As religious and spiritual persons we base our lives on an Ultimate Reality, and draw spiritual power and hope therefrom, in trust, in prayer or meditation, in word or silence. We have a special responsibility for the welfare of all humanity and care for the planet Earth. We do not consider ourselves better than other women and men, but we trust that the ancient wisdom of our religions can point the way for the future.

After two world wars and the end of the cold war, the collapse of fascism and nazism, the shaking to the foundations of communism and colonialism, humanity has entered a new phase of its history. Today we possess sufficient economic, cultural, and spiritual resources to introduce a better global order. But old and new ethnic, national, social, economic, and religious tensions threaten the peaceful building of a better world. We have experienced greater technological progress than ever before, yet we see that world-wide poverty, hunger, death of children, unemployment, misery, and the destruction of nature have not diminished but rather have increased. Many peoples are threatened with economic ruin, social disarray, political marginalization, ecological catastrophe, and national collapse.

In such a dramatic global situation humanity needs a vision of peoples living peacefully together, of ethnic and ethical groupings and of religions sharing responsibility for the care of Earth. A vision rests on hopes, goals, ideals, standards. But all over the world these have slipped from our hands. Yet we are convinced that, despite their frequent abuses and failures, it is the communities of faith who bear a responsibility to demonstrate that such hopes, ideals, and standards can be guarded, grounded, and lived. This is especially true in the modern state. Guarantees of freedom of conscience and religion are necessary but they do not substitute for binding values, convictions, and norms which are valid for all humans regardless of their social origin, sex, skin color, language, or religion.

We are convinced of the fundamental unity of the human family on Earth. We recall the 1948 Universal Declaration of Human Rights of the United Nations. What it formally proclaimed on the level of rights we wish to confirm and deepen here from the perspective of an ethic: The full realization of the intrinsic dignity of the human person, the inalienable freedom and equality in principle of all humans, and the necessary solidarity and interdependence of all humans with each other.

On the basis of personal experiences and the burdensome history of our planet we have learned

- that a better global order cannot be created or enforced by laws, prescriptions, and conventions alone;
- that the realization of peace, justice, and the protection of Earth depends on the insight and readiness of men and women to act justly;
- that action in favor of rights and freedoms presumes a consciousness of responsibility and duty, and that therefore both the minds and hearts of women and men must be addressed;
- that rights without morality cannot long endure, and that *there will be no better global order without a global ethic.*

By a global ethic we do not mean a global ideology or a single unified religion beyond all existing religions, and certainly not the domination of one religion over all others. By a global ethic we mean a fundamental consensus on binding values, irrevocable standards, and personal attitudes. Without such a fundamental consensus on an ethic, sooner or later every community will be threatened by chaos or dictatorship, and individuals will despair.

II. A fundamental demand: Every human being must be treated humanely

We are all fallible, imperfect men and women with limitations and defects. We know the reality of evil. Precisely because of this, we feel compelled for the sake of global welfare to express what the fundamental elements of a global ethic should be – for individuals as well as for communities and organizations, for states as well as for the religions themselves. We trust that our often millennia-old religious and ethical traditions provide an ethic which is convincing and practicable for all women and men of good will, religious and non-religious.

At the same time we know that our various religious and ethical traditions often offer very different bases for what is helpful and what is unhelpful for men and women, what is right and what is wrong, what is good and what is evil. We do not wish to gloss over or ignore the serious differences among the individual religions. However, they should not hinder us from proclaiming publicly those things which we already hold in common and which we jointly affirm, each on the basis of our own religious or ethical grounds.

We know that religions cannot solve the environmental, economic, political and social problems of Earth. However they can provide what obviously cannot be attained by economic plans, political programs, or legal regulations alone: A change in the inner orientation, the whole mentality, the 'hearts' of people, and a conversion from a false path to a new orientation for life. Humankind urgently needs social and ecological reforms, but it needs spiritual renewal just as urgently. As religious or spiritual persons we commit ourselves to this task. The spiritual powers of the religions can offer a fundamental sense of trust, a ground of meaning, ultimate standards, and a spiritual home. Of course religions are credible only when they eliminate those conflicts which spring from the religions themselves, dismantling mutual arrogance, mistrust, prejudice, and even hostile images, and thus demonstrate respect for the traditions, holy places, feasts, and rituals of people who believe differently.

Now as before, women and men are treated inhumanely all over the world. They are robbed of their opportunities and their freedom; their human rights are trampled underfoot; their dignity is disregarded. But might does not make right! In the face of all inhumanity our religious and ethical convictions demand that *every human being must be treated humanely!*

This means that every human being without distinction of age, sex, race, skin color, physical or mental ability, language, religion, political view, or national or social origin possess an inalienable and untouchable dignity, and everyone, the individual as well as the state, is therefore obliged to honor this dignity and protect it. Humans must always be the subjects of rights, must be ends, never mere means, never objects of commercialization and industrialization in economics, politics and media, in research institutes, and industrial corporations. No one stands 'above good and evil' – no human being, no social class, no influential interest group, no cartel, no police apparatus, no army, and no state. On the contrary: Possessed of reason and conscience, every human is obliged to behave in a genuinely human fashion, to do good and avoid evil!

It is the intention of this Global Ethic to clarify what this means. In it we wish to recall irrevocable, unconditional ethical norms. These should not be bonds and chains, but helps and supports for people to find and realize once again their lives' direction, values, orientations, and meaning.

There is a principle which is found and has persisted in many religious and ethical traditions of humankind for thousands of years: *What you do not wish done to yourself, do not do to others.* Or in positive terms: *What you wish done to yourself, do to others!* This should be the irrevocable, unconditional norm for all areas of life, for families and communities, for races, nations, and religions.

Every form of egoism should be rejected: All selfishness, whether individual or collective, whether in the form of class thinking, racism, nationalism, or sexism. We condemn these because they prevent humans from being authentically human. Self-determination and self-realization are thoroughly legitimate so long as they are not separated from human self-responsibility and global responsibility, that is, from responsibility for fellow humans and for the planet Earth.

This principle implies very concrete standards to which we humans should hold firm. From it arise four broad, ancient guidelines for human behavior which are found in most of the religions of the world.

III. Irrevocable directives

1. Commitment to a Culture of Non-violence and Respect for Life

Numberless women and men of all regions and religions strive to lead lives not determined by egoism but by commitment to their fellow humans and to the world around them. Nevertheless, all over the world we find endless hatred, envy, jealousy, and violence, not only between individuals but also between social and ethnic groups, between classes, races, nations, and religions. The use of violence, drug trafficking and organized crime, often equipped with new technical possibilities, has reached global proportions.

A Global Ethic

Many places are still ruled by terror 'from above'; dictators oppress their own people, and institutional violence is widespread. Even in some countries where laws exist to protect individual freedoms, prisoners are tortured, men and women are mutilated, hostages are killed.

a) In the great ancient religious and ethical traditions of humankind we find the directive: *You shall not kill!* Or in positive terms: *Have respect for life!* Let us reflect anew on the consequences of this ancient directive: All people have a right to life, safety, and the free development of personality insofar as they do not injure the rights of others. No one has the right physically or psychically to torture, injure, much less kill, any other human being. And no people, no state, no race, no religion has the right to hate, to discriminate against, to 'cleanse', to exile, much less to liquidate a 'foreign' minority which is different in behavior or holds different beliefs.

b) Of course, wherever there are humans there will be conflicts. Such conflicts, however, should be resolved without violence within a framework of justice. This is true for states as well as for individuals. Persons who hold political power must work within the framework of a just order and commit themselves to the most non-violent, peaceful solutions possible. And they should work for this within an international order of peace which itself has need of protection and defense against perpetrators of violence. Armament is a mistaken path; disarmament is the commandment of the times. Let no one be deceived: There is no survival for humanity without global peace!

c) Young people must learn at home and in school that violence may not be a means of settling differences with others. Only thus can a culture of non-violence be created.

d) A human person is infinitely precious and must be unconditionally protected. But likewise the lives of animals and plants which inhabit this planet with us deserve protection, preservation, and care. Limitless exploitation of the natural foundations of life, ruthless destruction of the biosphere, and militarization of the cosmos are all outrages. As human beings we have a special responsibility – especially with a view to future generations – for Earth and the cosmos, for the air, water, and soil. We are all intertwined together in this cosmos and we are all dependent on each other. Each one of us depends on the welfare of all. Therefore the dominance of humanity over nature and the cosmos must not be encouraged. Instead we must cultivate living in harmony with nature and the cosmos.

e) To be authentically human in the spirit of our great religious and ethical traditions means that in public as well as in private life we must be concerned for others and ready to help. We must never be ruthless and brutal. Every people, every race, every religion must show tolerance and respect – indeed high appreciation – for every other. Minorities need protection and support, whether they be racial, ethnic, or religious.

2. Commitment to a Culture of Solidarity and a Just Economic Order

Numberless men and women of all regions and religions strive to live their lives in solidarity with one another and to work for authentic fulfillment of their vocations. Nevertheless, all over the world we find endless hunger, deficiency, and need. Not only individuals, but especially unjust institutions and structures are responsible for these tragedies. Millions of people are without work; millions are exploited by poor wages, forced to the edges of society, with their possibilities for the future destroyed. In many lands the gap between the poor and the rich, between the powerful and the powerless is immense. We live in a world in which totalitarian state socialism as well as unbridled capitalism have hollowed out and destroyed many ethical and spiritual values. A materialistic mentality breeds greed for unlimited profit and a grasping for endless plunder. These demands claim more and more of the community's resources without obliging the individual to contribute more. The cancerous social evil of corruption thrives in the developing countries and in the developed countries alike.

a) In the great ancient religious and ethical traditions of humankind we find the directive: *You shall not steal!* Or in positive terms: *Deal honestly and fairly!* Let us reflect anew on the consequences of this ancient directive: No one has the right to rob or dispossess in any way whatsoever any other person or the commonweal. Further, no one has the right to use her or his possessions without concern for the needs of society and Earth.

b) Where extreme poverty reigns, helplessness and despair spread, and theft occurs again and again for the sake of survival. Where power and wealth are accumulated ruthlessly, feelings of envy, resentment, and deadly hatred and rebellion inevitably well up in the disadvantaged and marginalized. This leads to a vicious circle of violence and counter-violence. Let no one be deceived: There is no global peace without global justice!

c) Young people must learn at home and in school that property, limited though it may be, carries with it an obligation, and that its uses should at the same time serve the common good. Only thus can a just economic order be built up.

d) If the plight of the poorest billions of humans on this planet, particularly women and children, is to be improved, the world economy must be structured more justly. Individual good deeds, and assistance projects, indispensable though they be, are insufficient. The participation of all states and the authority of international organizations are needed to build just economic institutions.

A solution which can be supported by all sides must be sought for the debt crisis and the poverty of the dissolving second world, and even more the third world. Of course conflicts of interest are unavoidable. In the developed countries, a distinction must be made between necessary and limitless consumption, between socially beneficial and non-beneficial uses of property, between justified and unjustified uses of natural resources, and between a profit-only and a socially beneficial and ecologically oriented market economy. Even the developing nations must search their national consciences.

Wherever those ruling threaten to repress those ruled, wherever institutions threaten persons, and wherever might oppresses right, we are obligated to resist – whenever possible non-violently.

e) To be authentically human in the spirit of our great religious and ethical traditions means the following:

• We must utilize economic and political power for service to humanity instead of misusing it in ruthless battles for domination. We must develop a spirit of compassion with those who suffer, with special care for the children, the aged, the poor, the disabled, the refugees, and the lonely.

• We must cultivate mutual respect and consideration, so as to reach a reasonable balance of interests, instead of thinking only of unlimited power and unavoidable competitive struggles.

• We must value a sense of moderation and modesty instead of an unquenchable greed for money, prestige, and consumption. In greed humans lose their 'souls', their freedom, their composure, their inner peace, and thus that which makes them human.

3. Commitment to a Culture of Tolerance and a Life of Truthfulness

Numberless women and men of all regions and religions strive to lead lives of honesty and truthfulness. Nevertheless, all over the world we find endless lies and deceit, swindling and hypocrisy, ideology and demagoguery:

49

- Politicians and business people who use lies as a means to success;
- Mass media which spread ideological propaganda instead of accurate reporting, misinformation instead of information, cynical commercial interest instead of loyalty to the truth;
- Scientists and researchers who give themselves over to morally questionable ideological or political programs or to economic interest groups, or who justify research which violates fundamental ethical values;
- Representatives of religions who dismiss other religions as of little value and who preach fanaticism and intolerance instead of respect and understanding.

a) In the great ancient religious and ethical traditions of humankind we find the directive: *You shall not lie!* Or in positive terms: *Speak and act truthfully!* Let us reflect anew on the consequences of this ancient directive: No woman or man, no institution, no state or church or religious community has the right to speak lies to other humans.

b) This is especially true

- for those who work in the mass media, to whom we entrust the freedom to report for the sake of truth and to whom we thus grant the office of guardian. They do not stand above morality but have the obligation to respect human dignity, human rights, and fundamental values. They are duty-bound to objectivity, fairness, and the preservation of human dignity. They have no right to intrude into individuals' private spheres, to manipulate public opinion, or to distort reality;
- for artists, writers, and scientists, to whom we entrust artistic and academic freedom. They are not exempt from general ethical standards and must serve the truth;
- for the leaders of countries, politicians, and political parties, to whom we entrust our own freedoms. When they lie in the faces of their people, when they manipulate the truth, or when they are guilty of venality or ruthlessness in domestic or foreign affairs, they forsake their credibility and deserve to lose their offices and their voters. Conversely, public opinion should support those politicians who dare to speak the truth to the people at all times;
- finally, for representatives of religion. When they stir up prejudice, hatred, and enmity towards those of different belief, or even incite or legitimize religious wars, they deserve the condemnation of humankind and the loss of their adherents.

Let no one be deceived: There is no global justice without truthfulness and humaneness!

c) Young people must learn at home and in school to think, speak, and act truthfully. They have a right to information and education to be able to make the decisions that will form their lives. Without an ethical formation they will hardly be able to distinguish the important from the unimportant. In the daily flood of information, ethical standards will help them discern when opinions are portrayed as facts, interests veiled, tendencies exaggerated, and facts twisted.

d) To be authentically human in the spirit of our great religious and ethical traditions means the following:

- We must not confuse freedom with arbitrariness or pluralism with indifference to truth.
- We must cultivate truthfulness in all our relationships instead of dishonesty, dissembling, and opportunism.
- We must constantly seek truth and incorruptible sincerity instead of spreading ideological or partisan half-truths.
- We must courageously serve the truth and we must remain constant and trustworthy, instead of yielding to opportunistic accommodation to life.

4. Commitment to a Culture of Equal Rights and Partnership Between Men and Women

Numberless men and women of all regions and religions strive to live their lives in a spirit of partnership and responsible action in the areas of love, sexuality, and family. Nevertheless, all over the world there are condemnable forms of patriarchy, domination of one sex over the other, exploitation of women, sexual misuse of children, and forced prostitution. Too frequently, social inequities force women and even children into prostitution as a means of survival – particularly in less developed countries.

a) In the great ancient religious and ethical traditions of humankind we find the directive: *You shall not commit sexual immorality!* Or in positive terms: *Respect and love one another!* Let us reflect anew on the consequences of this ancient directive: No one has the right to degrade others to mere sex objects, to lead them into or hold them in sexual dependency.

b) We condemn sexual exploitation and sexual discrimination as one of the worst forms of human degradation. We have the duty to resist wherever the domination of one sex over the other is preached – even in the name of religious conviction; wherever sexual exploitation is tolerated, wherever prostitution is fostered or children are misused. Let no one be deceived: There is no authentic humaneness without a living together in partnership!

c) Young people must learn at home and in school that sexuality is not a negative, destructive, or exploitative force, but creative and affirmative. Sexuality as a life-affirming shaper of community can only be effective when partners accept the responsibilities of caring for one another's happiness.

d) The relationship between women and men should be characterized not by patronizing behavior or exploitation, but by love, partnership, and trustworthiness. Human fulfillment is not identical with sexual pleasure. Sexuality should express and reinforce a loving relationship lived by equal partners.

Some religions know the ideal of a voluntary renunciation of the full use of sexuality. Voluntary renunciation also can be an expression of identity and meaningful fulfillment.

e) The social institution of marriage, despite all its cultural and religious variety, is characterized by love, loyalty, and permanence. It aims at and should guarantee security and mutual support to husband, wife, and child. It should secure the rights of all family members.

All lands and cultures should develop economic and social relationships which will enable marriage and family life worthy of human beings, especially for older people. Children have a right of access to education. Parents should not exploit children, nor children parents. Their relationships should reflect mutual respect, appreciation, and concern.

f) To be authentically human in the spirit of our great religious and ethical traditions means the following:

- We need mutual respect, partnership, and understanding, instead of patriarchal domination and degradation, which are expressions of violence and engender counter-violence.
- We need mutual concern, tolerance, readiness for reconciliation, and love, instead of any form of possessive lust or sexual misuse.

Only what has already been experienced in personal and familial relationships can be practiced on the level of nations and religions.

IV. A Transformation of Consciousness!

Historical experience demonstrates the following: Earth cannot be changed for the better unless we achieve a transformation in the consciousness of individuals and in public life. The possibilities for transformation have already been glimpsed in areas such as war and peace, economy, and ecology, where in recent decades fundamental changes have taken place. This transformation must also be achieved in the area of ethics and values!

Every individual has intrinsic dignity and inalienable rights, and each also has an inescapable responsibility for what she or he does and does not do. All our decisions and deeds, even our omissions and failures, have consequences.

Keeping this sense of responsibility alive, deepening it and passing it on to future generations, is the special task of religions.

We are realistic about what we have achieved in this consensus, and so we urge that the following be observed:

1. A universal consensus on many disputed ethical questions (from bio- and sexual ethics through mass media and political ethics) will be difficult to attain. Nevertheless, even for many controversial questions, suitable solutions should be attainable in the spirit of the fundamental principles we have jointly developed here.

2. In many areas of life a new consciousness of ethical responsibility has already arisen. Therefore we would be pleased if as many professions as possible, such as those of physicians, scientists, business people, journalists, and politicians, would develop up-to-date codes of ethics which would provide specific guidelines for the vexing questions of these particular professions.

3. Above all, we urge the various communities of faith to formulate their very specific ethics: What does each faith tradition have to say, for example, about the meaning of life and death, the enduring of suffering and the forgiveness of guilt, about selfless sacrifice and the necessity of renunciation, about compassion and joy. These will deepen, and make more specific, the already discernible global ethic.

In conclusion, we appeal to all the inhabitants of this planet. Earth cannot be changed for the better unless the consciousness of individuals is changed. We pledge to work for such transformation in individual and collective consciousness, for the awakening of our spiritual powers through reflection, meditation, prayer, or positive thinking, for a conversion of the heart. Together we can move mountains! Without a willingness to take risks and a readiness to sacrifice there can be no fundamental change in our situation! Therefore we commit ourselves to a common global ethic, to better mutual understanding, as well as to socially beneficial, peace-fostering, and Earth-friendly ways of life.

We invite all men and women, whether religious or not, to do the same.

A tale of three cities
The Rede Lecture 1993

DR L. M. SINGHVI

I

I consider it a great honour and a rare privilege to be appointed by the Vice-Chancellor of Cambridge University to the ancient office created by Sir Robert Rede's executors by a deed of 10 December 1524.

I join the distinguished galaxy of my illustrious predecessors with utmost hesitation but at the same time with the greatest pleasure. I recall the story of two bishops, one of whom introduced the other to an audience freely using hyperbole in praising him. When the other bishop rose to speak, he said he had two apologies to make: one apology on behalf of his friend, the bishop who introduced him with a profusion of superlatives, because the friendly bishop had exceeded the bounds of truth. The other apology, he said, was on his own behalf – for enjoying what the other bishop had said in his praise. I think I might also make two apologies, one on behalf of the Vice-Chancellor for his error of choice and the other on my own behalf for enjoying it so much.

Lord Denning told me once that, as a lawyer, he derived particular pleasure (as a judge he called it wicked pleasure), when he undeservedly won a case which lacked merit. As to the merit of the present speaker, I shall say nothing, but I am in a position to testify that Lord Denning was quite right about a certain pleasure in undeserved gain. I might add the postscript *nota bene* that there is no wickedness whatever in my own delight in receiving this much valued academic distinction. The fault evidently is attributable to an error of judgement and the blame for it can be laid squarely at the doors of the distinguished Vice-Chancellor. I reckon I need no other alibi for making bold to come to you this evening, armed as I am with my appointment by the Vice-Chancellor which gives me my credentials to claim the audience of this august assembly.

In fairness to the Vice-Chancellor, I must tell you that I have been treated far better by him than was Sir Robert Rede by King Henry VII who appointed him as the Chief Justice of Common Pleas in the year 1506. I have learnt on good authority that the avaricious King Henry VII asked for and obtained from his appointee, namely Sir Robert Rede, a sum of 400 marks, equivalent to about 3,200 ounces of silver. Sir David Williams, who appointed me, not only did not ask me for any marks, sterling or precious metal, but true to the justly acclaimed traditions of Welsh warmth, offered me his hospitality. Lest the Vice-Chancellor should feel that he missed an opportunity, I should remind him that, unlike him, King Henry VII did not ask Sir Robert Rede to give lectures as prescribed in *Statuta Antiqua* on Humanity, Logic and Philosophy or on Physics and Metaphysics of Aristotle. Nor am I holding the Master and Fellows of Jesus College responsible under the ancient endowment for the payment of the stipulated sum of £4 to me from the common chest. Suffice it to remind ourselves in that context that Sir Robert Rede, may his soul rest in peace, was the first to give a fixed stipend to the lecturers and thus pioneered the concept of solicitous concern for the lecturing academics who might otherwise have to share their predicament with the proverbial church mice whose exact function and warrant of authority for their presence in the churches I have never been able to understand. I might add, *en passant* and by way of comparison, that the temple mice in India lead a comparatively more rewarding and prosperous life.

Venturing to lecture to those who live by lecturing or whose staple diet consists of listening to appetising lectures day after day is the most daunting task one can undertake. My plea for what may appear to be either indiscretion or zealous valour is simply that the temptation was irresistible and sometimes the best way to overcome a temptation is to yield to it. I confess I have done it before and given the opportunity I shall perhaps do it again. I do not mind revealing to you what I think may be the hidden reason for this streak of recklessness in me. The reason I suspect is that a little less than four decades ago I abandoned an academic career which was my first love and opted for the more lucrative profession of a practising lawyer, although not entirely because it was more lucrative. Ever since, I have suffered from frequent bouts of nostalgia and occasional pangs of conscience. Returning to the academic profession, howsoever temporarily, is for me at once an excursion and an expiation. Perhaps, going to one's first love by stealth in the sanctuary of a great University, away from Diplomacy, a jealous mistress like my lifelong profession of Law, has its own romance. Romance, after all, is always where you were, not where you are. But Sir Robert Rede would have had none of it. I hear the solemn and far-reaching voice of his executors that these lectures 'shall be for ever read franc and free to all manner of schollers of the said Vniversitie hearing or bounde to hear the same'. I do not know if anyone ever was or is 'bounde to hear' the Rede lectures except those who are present of their own volition. As to the requirement of giving a frank and free lecture, I can only promise to do my best even if I have to betray what are assumed to be the rules of the diplomatic game which is commonly and somewhat erroneously taken to be wholly devious rather than frank. In any event, by natural disposition I prefer to be frank and free, and being a lawyer by training and profession and a rank outsider in the realm of diplomacy, I have no difficulty in following the injunction of Sir Robert Rede's executors to be frank and free.

My difficulty was not with the directions stipulated by Sir Robert Rede's executors but with those who had been chosen in previous years to carry out the mandate. To deliver the Rede Lecture in succession to the great philosopher-poet John Ruskin (1867), Professor Max Mueller (1868), Professor Frederick W. Maitland (1901), Sir Francis Younghusband (1905), Mathew Arnold (1882), The Earl Curzon (1913), HRH Prince Philip, the Chancellor of

Cambridge University (1979) and Lord Jenkins of Hillhead, the Chancellor of Oxford University (1988), to name only a few of my predecessors after 1859, appeared to me to be palpably presumptuous. Indeed, they were all so distinguished that I experienced considerable discomfiture in accepting the appointment and was in awe even while basking in their reflected glory. Reading the list of names and some of the Rede lectures which were so kindly made available to me by kind friends in Cambridge, the realisation of what I had undertaken to do finally dawned upon me. By then it was too late for me to backtrack. On the other hand, the more I thought about it, the more difficult the task appeared to me.

What seemed most difficult to me was the choice of the subject. First I thought of delivering a lecture on East and West in the hope that I could do 'poetic' justice to Rudyard Kipling and also make the twain meet. Numerous alternatives and several months later, when I finally decided to caption my lecture as 'A tale of three cities', my wife thought I was about to lapse into spinning a yarn beginning with the city of my birth, Jodhpur, and indulge in autobiographical or ancestral anecdotage which she associates with dotage. Of course, she came to that conclusion without giving me an opportunity of explaining to her what I had in mind for, as we all know, it is the wont and prerogative of spouses, particularly wives, not to be bothered about observing the elementary rules of fair play and natural justice so admirably and elaborately expounded by Professor Sir William Wade in his *magnum opus* on Administrative Law.

Without making the short story long and my preamble as long as the lecture, let me disclose to you that I have in mind Rio, Vienna and Chicago as my three cities for this lecture, and that entirely because during about fifteen months, from June 1992 to September 1993, three major world conferences were held in those cities and they became symbolic of global concerns and aspirations, first in respect of Environment and Sustainable Development, secondly, Human Rights, and lastly Inter-faith Dialogue and Harmony. The tale this evening unfolds itself in those three cities but is intertwined by a continuity of shared contemporary challenges and responses.

A tale of three cities

The title of my lecture, 'A Tale of Three Cities' is quite explicitly an unrepentant and plagiarised adaptation of *A Tale of Two Cities* by Charles Dickens which was published in 1859, the very year in which the Rede lectures were reorganised, 335 years after they had been established. The Dickensian tale of two cities (about London and Paris) begins in the year 1775. It portrays the upheaval of the French Revolution and the epic of the life of the ordinary struggling people in Houndsditch, the Old Bailey, St Antoine and Versailles during the terribly turbulent time of the early 1790s. As Dickens put it, 'It was the best of times, it was the worst of times, it was the age of wisdom, it was the age of foolishness, it was the epoch of belief, it was the epoch of incredulity, it was the season of Light, it was the season of Darkness, it was the spring of Hope, it was the winter of despair . . .'

Charles Dickens was one of the greatest storytellers of all times. I have none of that creativity and shall not attempt to emulate or imitate him. My tale of three cities which belongs to our own time is quite simply told, although in its plot and theme the elemental force of an epic story is not lacking.

The tale I wish to tell you is not a tale of the times gone by, not a fictional tale told in the past tense. It is in fact a tale of the tension of tenses and bridges between past, present and future. It contains fragments from the dreams and nightmares of humankind in the last decade of the twentieth century. It is not what the male chauvinists of yesteryear – I hope there are no more left – would have called an old wives' tale. It is not a tale of a tub or a tabloid tale. It does not qualify to be called a rigmarole. Nor is it a Robin Hood or Canterbury tale. I confess it is somewhat longwinded, but it is an honest tale, and if it is grim in parts, it is also promising and cheering in parts. Shakespeare thought that an honest tale speeds best being plainly told, although I should warn you that it takes a Shakespeare to achieve that result. I should try to speed my tale by telling it as plainly, simply and truthfully as possible. That will make my product quite academic and exclusive though not quite marketable because plainly workaday truths relating to the human condition, without salacious intrusions into someone's privacy, are not in vogue, perhaps never have been. I may tell you what a journalist said a few years ago in an erstwhile Iron Curtain country. He said with disarming candour: 'Well, our newspapers, like newspapers in the rest of the world, contain truths, half-truths and lies. The truths are in the sports pages, the half-truths in the weather forecasts, and lies everywhere else.' Under that classification, my tale of three cities would, I hope, belong to the sports pages.

II

The first city in my tale is Rio de Janeiro, the venue of the Earth Summit in June 1992. The Earth Summit was concerned with Human Survival and the protection of Planet Earth. It was concerned with designing a development process for the world as a whole that may not imperil its ecological balance. The second city is Vienna which hosted the UN World Conference on Human Rights in June 1993. It was concerned with Human Dignity without which Human Survival and Development would be devoid of their *raison d'être*. The third city in my tale is Chicago, where the centennial of the First Parliament of World's Religions of 1893 was commemorated in late August and early September 1993 and a declaration 'Towards a Global Ethic' was adopted and proclaimed. The Chicago Parliament of World's Religions was meant to put the issues of Human Survival, Sustainable Development and Human Dignity as well as the civilisational responses to the aberrations of Intolerance, Fanaticism and Violence in a shared ethical and spiritual perspective. My tale this evening is a tale of the three cities where the world community had gathered to address those issues and themes in June 1992, June 1993 and August–September 1993.

The tale of the first of my three cities did not really begin in Rio. Nor did it begin with the UN Conference on Environment and Development also known as Earth Summit in June 1992. It had begun ever since and each time human beings perceived their shared tenancy of Planet Earth, their membership of the human family and their common future. And it is an endless tale. In a sense it began in 1972 in Stockholm which was quite unlike Rio. The seeds for the harvest in Rio were sown in Stockholm. In twenty years, the propitious and somewhat modest beginning made in Stockholm had become a mighty movement enlivened by a new-found sense of the oneness of our world and its common future.

There are those who believe that the perception of the oneness of our world may have dawned upon us in the middle of the twentieth century when we saw our planet from space for the first time with the eyes and cameras of our astronauts. Seeing Planet Earth from space was certainly more revolutionary than the Copernican revolution of the sixteenth century, but the idea of one world and the whole world as one family was certainly much older. Indian and Greek thought was, for instance, suffused with a strikingly refreshing sense of universality. Trackless centuries ago, Indian philosophers had declared, in words the meaning of which is as modern as the day after tomorrow, and that declaration freely rendered from Sanskrit verse would be as follows:

> It is the small-minded who trivialize this world by their preoccupation with many kinds of divisions and demarcations which separate the peoples of the world. Those who are generous of spirit and have a larger vision regard the whole world as one family.

Obviously, the divisions and demarcations which separate the peoples of the world as well as their sense of shared heritage which unites them are both equally real. Tragically, what is more compelling and real today is that in the age of the greatest affluence and advancement in the history of human civilisation, the world, our one and only world, may be on the brink of disaster, devastation and destruction. That was the alarm signal on the agenda of the Earth Summit at Rio.

The Report of the World Commission on Environment and Development titled 'Our Common Future' had pointed out in 1987 lapses of environmental neglect and degradation and the perils of developmental failures. It pointed out that in terms of absolute numbers there were more hungry people in the world than ever before; their numbers were increasing even though global food production had increased faster than the population growth. It pointed out that the numbers of those who could not read or write, of those without safe water or safe and sound homes, and of those who lacked fuel to cook and warm themselves were increasing and the gap between the rich and poor nations was widening. It also pointed out that each year some 6 million hectares of productive dryland was turning into worthless desert and more than 11 million hectares of forests were destroyed. During the 1970s, twice as many people suffered each year from natural disasters as during the 1960s. In the 1960s, some 18.5 million people were affected annually by drought and 5.2 million by floods; in the 1970s correspondingly 24.4 million and 15.4 million people were affected annually. Numbers of victims of cyclones and earthquakes also increased considerably. Worse still, we have persisted in a profligate use of Earth's finite resources and have continued to precipitate global warming and climate change by excessive burning of fossil fuels, denude the first cover of the Earth, cause desertification and extreme scarcity of water, necessitate shifting of agricultural areas, raise sea levels, flood coastal cities, submerge low-lying islands and disrupt national economies. Pollution is rampant. There is a criminal dumping of industrial waste. The planet's protective ozone shield is on the brink of depletion. Toxic substances poison the human food chain and the underground water tables. The world's bio-diversity is being progressively destroyed. We have already transgressed the tolerance limits of benign Nature and the dangers are clear and present. As the UN Commission had concluded, the environmental crisis, the development crisis and the energy crisis are all one and the crisis is global. The crisis can no longer be contained in national compartments or labelled under neat traditional classifications.

The UN Commission proposed a strategy of Sustainable Development which aimed 'to promote harmony among human beings and between humanity and nature'. In the blueprint presented to the Earth Summit at Rio, Sustainable Development emerged as the new composite creed of environment and development, a new creative discipline for survival, growth, adjustments, equity, flexibility, innovation, sharing and togetherness. This was the approach of common sense to our common future at the Earth Summit. The Rio Declaration and Agenda 21 adopted at Rio sought to embody that approach.

The Rio Declaration boldly establishes two basic principles: first, that human beings are at the centre of concerns for sustainable development and are entitled to a healthy and productive life in harmony with nature, not merely as objects, recipients and beneficiaries, but as participants in the process; and secondly, that Peace, Development and Environmental Protection are inter-dependent and indivisible. The Rio Declaration emphasises cooperation 'in a spirit of partnership to conserve, protect and restore the health and integrity of the Earth's ecosystem'. Significantly, the philosophical principle underlying the Rio Declaration is the principle of harmony and not adversarial confrontation with or forcible conquest of Nature. It seems to me that this is a fundamental cultural concession by the West in its interaction with the East, or perhaps the West has rediscovered St Francis of Assisi after a long and tortuous journey.

The Rio Declaration accepts the sovereign right of States to exploit their own resources pursuant to their own policies, but clearly limits that right by their responsibility to ensure that their activities do not cause damage to the environment of other States or of areas beyond the limits of national jurisdiction. The clear enunciation of the principle of international responsibility in the twin fields of Environment and Development is a valuable conceptual con-tribution underpinning the emerging jurisprudence of international accountability. Two other major dimensions of accountability are embodied in the Declaration: the principle of inter-generational equity; and the principle of responsibility of all States and all people 'to cooperate in the task of eradicating poverty as an indispensable requirement for sustainable development, in order to decrease the disparities in standards of living and better meet the needs of the majority of the people of the world'. A third cognate equitable principle is to accord special priority to 'the special situation and needs of developing countries, particularly the least developed and those most environmentally vulnerable'. Finally, the most vital equitable aspect of the Rio Declaration is the unqualified acknowledgement by the developed countries of the responsibility they bear in the international pursuit of sustainable development in view of the pressures their societies place on the global environment and of the technologies and financial resources they command.

If I wanted to parade a whole battalion of principles, precepts and programmes on Environment and Development, I could go on to elaborate and annotate all the twenty-seven Principles embodied in the Rio Declaration and to summarise all the overlapping forty chapters under Agenda 21. That would only demonstrate that the Earth Summit in Rio was long on words but short on allocation of resources and shorter still on the means of actual implementation. We thought we had come a long way from Stockholm in June 1972 to Rio in June 1992, but I had a disconcerting feeling that in the deafening rhetoric of Rio, the dialogue itself was lost or submerged.

The principal achievement of Rio, no doubt, was an enormous increase in public awareness of the issues and of the stakes involved in sustainable development. It also secured a set of agreements between governments and won a measure of political commitment to the Principles and the Agenda. It was however disappointing in operational terms, particularly in the context of the urgency and the magnitude of the problems of survival and the hopes and expectations it had aroused. Rio gave us guiding norms and a sense of direction but it failed to give us an effective and comprehensive international legal framework and a functional knitting together of Environment and Development, Ecology and Economics, Equity and Empowerment.

One might draw some comfort from Richard Sandbrook's observation that 'this is itself a mammoth step forward as politicians come to understand that the issues do not just concern plants and animals but life itself . But that sense of comfort is not durable when we find that the world, predominantly the industrially advanced countries of the world, continue to push more than 7 billion metric tons per year of carbon dioxide into the atmosphere. The Rio Principles and Agenda 21 do represent a way forward and do therefore offer a measure of hope but you cannot for long stroke people with mere words and console them with hope, not when the threat to life and civilisation looms large upon the world. Rio was no doubt a spectacular mega event, by far the largest UN Conference ever held. There were close to 10,000 official delegates from 150 or more countries and perhaps 15,000 concerned citizens and activists participating in a parallel Global Forum. About 7,000 journalists were accredited to the Conference. As many as 116 national political leaders attended the Rio Summit. For all that fanfare, it failed to achieve a real, comprehensive and credible Action Plan fully backed by resources, legal mechanisms and political will. What Rio failed to accomplish was to secure compliance with the Rio Principles and for translating Agenda 21 into a living reality. In that sense, Rio was a missed opportunity and the danger therefore is that the Rio Principles may remain in the glasscase and Agenda 21 in the cupboard!

The real problem at Rio was the North–South divide which often seemed to obscure, even eclipse, the immediate and practical objectives of the Earth Summit. Both the North and the South failed to rise above the divide. They haggled but failed to strike a bargain. The affluent North failed to rise to the occasion. The great discourse which had begun at Stockholm had perhaps lost its inspiration and momentum somewhere along the line. The summiteers played their armchair game of chess; they did not band together to climb and scale the heights as one team. With all the concentration of political power, economic and financial resources, scientific knowledge and skills in the North, the moral vision of the North flagged and faltered. At the end of the day, the world got its Rio Declaration, its Agenda 21, two conventions and a set of guidelines, but that was woefully inadequate to save the Planet Earth from imminent perils. The North acknowledged what it owed but it was not prepared to pay. It accepted what it must do to change its lifestyle and consumption levels but was not prepared to make a commitment or even the beginning of a credible attempt. A level playing field was not yet ready. Environment and Development were practising separately as players but their working partnership which was the name of the game and which was at the heart of the agenda of the Earth Summit had not yet begun.

III

Exactly a year after Rio, nearly 180 nations went to Vienna for the UN World Human Rights Conference in June 1993. The preparatory process for the Vienna Conference which started in December 1990 included the UN Conferences held in Tunis, San José and Bangkok. A conference was also held at Strasbourg to preview the issues on the agenda of the Vienna Conference.

At Vienna, we were not really breaking new ground. In that respect, Vienna was quite different from Rio. As compared to Rio, we had many more options and many more building blocks to work with in Vienna. A quarter century after the Teheran Conference on Human Rights in 1968 and some forty-five years after the Universal Declaration was proclaimed by the General Assembly of the United Nations, there was already a functioning human rights framework within the UN system. The perceived role and prescribed purpose of the Conference at Vienna were less ambitious than those of the Earth Summit at Rio. The task of the Vienna Conference was mainly to carry out a comprehensive analysis of the international human rights system and of the machinery for the protection of human rights in order to enhance and thus promote a fuller observance of those rights in a just and balanced manner.

Throughout the preparatory process preceding Vienna, one could hear dire prophecies of fatal ideological, political and cultural cleavages which were bound to lead to the collapse of the Conference. It was predicted that the Conference could not produce an agreed document because no agreement could be reached between

the North and the South and the East and the West on most of the
vital issues relating to human rights. Why did we need a World
Conference?, asked some. At any rate, why did we need an
agreed document at the end of the Conference?, asked many in
exasperation.

The sledgehammer warnings and the bleak and gloomy
predictions were misconceived. In fact, the media took little notice
of the vital bridging role many countries in the East and the West
were playing to achieve consensus at the successive stages of the
preparatory process. I am proud to say that India was in the forefront
of that constructive endeavour. Media, however, picked up only the
more negative aspects in the consultative process leading to Vienna.
We were told by the media chorus that the Asians challenged the very
concept of human rights and that the West could not accept the
Right to Development as a human right and denied the indivisibility
of civil, political, economic, social and cultural human rights. We
were also informed that the non-Western States of the United
Nations wanted to abrogate the idea of the universality of human
rights and make them wholly culture-specific. I am glad to say that
Vienna successfully belied the prophets of doom and gloom.

Let me for a moment transport you to the Conference Centre. In
the main hall on the top floor, we met in the plenary sessions where
each national delegation delivered its prepared text. A wag said that
in the plenary we were playing either to the global gallery or to the
gallery at home. Largely true, but one need not be too apologetic
about playing to the gallery in our democratic age. It was at the
ground level, in the conference hall, in lunch rooms, in corridors and
in the lounges, which escaped or eluded close media attention, that
the diplomatic dialectics of the drafting exercise took place in which
we negotiated the texts. That process was too complex, perhaps too
monotonous and too hair-splitting or head-splitting, to interest the
media and the casual observers. In the basement of the Conference
Centre, there were countless Non-Governmental Organisations,
most of them constructive, well-intentioned and reasonable, a few
raucous, agitated and strident – and all of them saying different

things at the same time. Most of them had their friendly sympathisers and spokesmen on the ground floor. The channels of communication between the basement floor and the ground floor were quite good. To the outside visitor at the Conference Centre, I am afraid, we did seem often enough to have outdone the Tower of Babel. No wonder we had such a bad press, but even that had its positive chastening and salutary effect on the chemistry of the Conference. Midway through the Conference, we began working late nights, sometimes until the early hours of the morning, and discovered that the Conference fatigue and exhaustion was a great catalyst of proven efficacy to bring about a meeting of minds. Perhaps, the media pundits had not reckoned with such imponderable providential inputs. Nor had they made allowances for the ubiquitous principle that every conference worth the name had to have one or more problematic areas, and a global conference with some 180 countries participating had to have at least 180 problems. In the event, we solved most of them without any major mishap and produced a Declaration and Programme of Action which was adopted unanimously on the concluding day.

The Vienna Declaration and Programme of Action is no doubt a document of certain compromises, but there is in it no compromise on essentials. It is not as inspiring and evocative as the Universal Declaration on Human Rights; it is not as precise and terse as the Covenant on Civil and Political Rights and other treaty documents, but it is a document which in its elaborate Preamble, thirty-nine declaratory paragraphs in Part I followed by another 100 paragraphs of norms and recommendations consolidates human rights jurisprudence, contains a welcome restatement of the law and practice on the widest possible range of human rights issues, and reflects a remarkable balance and objectivity on human rights issues. It does not solve all the conceptual and operational human rights dilemmas the world faces today. The document has the Fabian virtue of perseverance and occasionally employs the Fabian tactics of avoiding direct engagements and confrontations. Admittedly, it had nothing meaningful to offer on Bosnia, geographically almost next door to

Vienna. Nor was it the purpose and mandate of the Vienna Conference to address and resolve specific country issues. The Vienna Conference has to be judged on the touchstone of what it was called upon to do and on that basis it was a reasonable, if not a resounding, success. To borrow from a preambular paragraph of the Vienna Declaration which I was privileged to draft, the Vienna Conference did seek to invoke the human rights spirit of our age and did endeavour to reflect the realities of our time.

The fundamental postulate and the starting point of the Vienna Declaration is that all human rights derive from the dignity and worth inherent in the human person and that the human person is the central subject of human rights and fundamental freedoms. The Declaration establishes a clear conceptual concordance between Democracy, Development and Human Rights and calls upon the international community to support, strengthen and promote democracy, development and respect for human rights and fundamental freedoms in the entire world. It declares those concepts to be universal and unconditional. The principle is further elaborated in paragraph 8 of the Declaration which clearly declares: 'Democracy, development and respect for human rights and fundamental freedoms are interdependent and mutually reinforcing.'

The Declaration reaffirms the Right to Development as a universal and inalienable right and as an integral part of fundamental human rights. It seeks to strike a balance by stating in the same breath that development facilitates the enjoyment of all human rights but the lack of development may not be invoked to justify the abridgement of internationally recognised human rights. One can see a lurking contradiction in that formulation. If development facilitates the enjoyment of human rights, lack of it necessarily denies enjoyment of human rights. Poverty and privation inexorably corrode and erode human rights and become an objective explanation if not a justification for the neglect of human rights and human dignity in a given society.

The Declaration provides that the right to development shall be fulfilled so as to meet equitably developmental and environmental needs of present and future generations. It emphasises effective development policies at the national level as well as equitable economic relations and favourable economic environment at the international level. It calls upon the international community to make all efforts to help alleviate the external debt burden of developing countries. It affirms that extreme poverty and social exclusion constitute a violation of human dignity and stresses the need to promote the human rights of the poor and to put an end to extreme poverty and social exclusion. Great emphasis is placed by the Declaration on the protection and promotion of the human rights of all vulnerable sections in the society.

The Declaration provides in unambiguous terms that all human rights, civil, political, social, economic and cultural, are universal, indivisible and interrelated. Yet another conundrum controversy accentuating the theoretical North–South East–West controversy was thus quietly laid to rest by that simple declaration, which also calls upon the international community to treat all human rights globally in a fair and equal manner on the same footing and with the same emphasis, although in practical terms such equality is seldom feasible. The Declaration also wisely and discreetly recognises the significance of national and regional particularities and various historical, cultural and religious backgrounds without accepting that States may pick and choose certain rights and disregard others.

The World Conference pointedly declared that the speedy and comprehensive elimination of all forms of racism and racial discrimination, xenophobia and related intolerance was a priority task and called upon governments and the international community to take effective measures to prevent and combat them. It also declared that the acts, methods and practices of terrorism in all its forms and manifestations as well as linkage in some countries with drug trafficking are activities aimed at the destruction of human rights, fundamental freedoms and democracy, threatening territorial integrity and security of States and destabilising legitimately constituted governments.

The Declaration reiterates the human rights of women and of the girl child and welcomes the early ratification of the Convention on the Rights of the Child and the recognition of the human rights of children in the World Declaration on the Survival, Protection and Development of Children.

The Vienna Declaration emphasises the importance of the promotion and protection of the rights of persons belonging to minorities and reaffirms the obligation of States to ensure the observance of these rights without any discrimination and in full equality before the law, in accordance with the Declaration of the Rights of Persons belonging to National or Ethnic, Religious and Linguistic Minorities.

The World Conference was dismayed at massive violations of human rights especially in the form of genocide, ethnic cleansing and systematic rape of women in war situations creating mass exodus of refugees and displaced persons; it also expressed its dismay and condemnation of torture and cruel, inhuman treatment or punishment, summary and arbitrary executions, disappearance, arbitrary detentions, all forms of racism, racial discrimination and apartheid, foreign occupation and alien domination, xenophobia, poverty, hunger and other denials of economic, social and cultural rights, religious intolerance, terrorism, discrimination against women, and lack of the rule of law.

The Vienna Conference reaffirmed the important and constructive role played by national institutions for the promotion and protection of human rights and recognised that it is the right of each State to choose the framework which is best suited to its particular needs at the national level. It also recognised the important role of non-governmental organisations in the promotion of all human rights and in humanitarian activities at national, regional and international levels.

The Vienna Conference represented a periodic audit of human rights norms and mechanisms. It involved a rough and ready stock-taking and to that extent it was useful. Perhaps a more intensive and indepth analysis and evaluation would have been not only a scholar's delight but would also have served the processes of human rights standard-setting and policy-making in future. The Conference and the preparatory process helped to highlight the central importance of human needs, human rights and human obligations and the deep inter-relationship between moral perceptions, legal norms, economic conditions, cultural contexts and political configurations.

At the Conference, we often felt hamstrung by the politics of human rights but often enough it was through the politics of human rights that we managed to resolve deadlocks and come out of our blues and blind alleys. There was a curious mixture of the politics of hope and despair, of poverty and affluence, of pride and prejudice, of national sovereignty and international accountability, of hegemony and autonomy, and of regional, religious and secular interests and combinations. The end of the cold war was amply in evidence but so were the new uncertainties. The nation state was not about to become extinct. We could see new cooperative adjustments in the concept of sovereignty internationally and in regional groupings. The West or the North acted much more as a block than did Asia, Africa or Latin America, but it was not as if Alice had arrived in the Wonderland of an unipolar world under the US banner. At the same time, we were conscious that in the global animal farm, some nations are more equal than others. Nevertheless, numbers did count. So did persuasion, background knowledge, sincerity of purpose, and drafting and negotiating skills. There was also a certain diplomatic *esprit de corps* and a certain intellectual openness at Vienna which made the Conference much more of a diplomatic conference and because of which some of the sharpest edges of political angularities could be rubbed off and rounded. There was also an awareness that in fact a great deal had been achieved in the field of human rights in pursuance of the Charter of the United Nations and the Universal Declaration of Human Rights and enormous and exponential progress had been made in setting standards and in extending and broadening the frontiers of international accountability. At the same time, the world community was chastened by the thought that we had only made a modest beginning, that we had many promises to keep. We therefore put forward at Vienna a solid phalanx of concrete suggestions to secure progressively better implementation of human rights. None of us at Vienna thought that a human rights millennium was around the corner. Each one of us knew that there were many remaining areas of darkness at noon around the world. But there was hope and confidence.

IV

Let us now travel on the last leg of our transcontinental journey from Vienna to Chicago where a Parliament of the World's Religions was convened from 28 August to 5 September 1993. The 1993 Parliament of the World's Religions was a centennial commemoration of the first Parliament of the World's Religions held in Chicago in 1893, which was a unique event.

During the 100 years after the historic event in 1893, the world continued to be afflicted by religious intolerance, hatred and disharmony. The question we asked ourselves at Chicago was: Did the world's religions have a healing role to play? We were compelled to reflect with C. C. Colton who said: 'Men will wrangle for religion; write for it; fight for it; anything but live for it.'

The 1993 Parliament of the World's Religions was not a world conference of the nations of the world. It was not a conference representing State power. It was a conference of different faith communities at which were represented all the major religions of the world, many of them at the highest level. Religious and spiritual leaders from all over the world came to it to make common cause in securing peace, harmony and understanding. More than 7,000 delegates from all parts of the world congregated and proclaimed the essential unity of all religions. For nine days, the Parliament discussed innumerable issues relating principally to inter-faith dialogue in hundreds of meetings and finally the Assembly of Religious and Spiritual Leaders proclaimed an inter-faith declaration which was based on a two-year consultation among several hundred scholars and theologians representing the world's communities of faith. The title of the declaration is 'Towards a Global Ethic', and it opens with the cry of the heart: 'The world is in agony.' The Declaration laments: 'Peace eludes us . . . the planet is being destroyed . . . neighbours live in fear . . . women and men are estranged from each other . . . children die!' The Declaration condemns the abuse of the Earth's ecosystems. It condemns 'poverty that stifles life's potential; the hunger that weakens the human body; the economic disparities that threaten so many families with ruin'. It condemns 'the social disarray of the nations; the disregard of justice which pushes citizens to the margin; the anarchy overtaking our communities; and the insane death of children from violence'. In particular, it condemns aggression and hatred in the name of religion.

The 1993 Parliament of the World's Religions declares that there already exists the basis for a global ethic which offers the possibility of better individual and global order, and leads individuals away from despair and society away from chaos. It affirms that a common set of core values is found in the teaching of the religions and that these form the basis of a global ethic. It declares that the ancient guidelines for human behaviour found in the teachings of the religions of the world are the condition for a 'sustainable world order'. It declares: 'We are interdependent! Each of us depends on the well-being of the whole and so we have respect for the community of living beings, for people, animals and plants and for the preservation of earth, air, water and soil.' It counsels a commitment to respect life and dignity, individuality and diversity so that every person is treated humanely, without exception. It says: 'Opening our hearts to one another, we must sink our narrow differences for the cause of the world community, practicing a culture of solidarity and relatedness.' It emphasises that Earth cannot change for the better unless the consciousness of individuals is changed first, unless we strive for a just social and economic order, in which everyone has an equal chance to reach full potential as a human being. It declares: 'We commit ourselves to a culture of non-violence, respect, justice and peace. We shall not oppress, injure, torture or kill other human beings, forsaking violence as a means of settling differences.'

The Declaration towards a Global Ethic proclaims certain simple, seminal ideas which cannot be dismissed as mere pious platitudes or starry-eyed Utopian day-dreaming. Those ideas are basic and elemental. Without them, without a new global ethic, no new global order is possible. The message of Chicago is that our different religions and cultural traditions must not prevent our common involvement in opposing all forms of inhumanity and working for greater humaneness; that humanity needs a vision of peoples living peacefully together, of ethnic and ethical groupings and of religions sharing responsibility for the care of Earth; that the fundamental unity of human family on Earth must be the root conviction; that action in favour of rights and freedom presumes a consciousness of responsibility and duty and that therefore both the minds and hearts of women and men must be addressed; that the realisation of peace, justice and the protection of Earth depends on the insight and readiness of men and women to act justly; and that rights without morality cannot long endure.

The first fundamental demand of Global Ethic is that every human being must be treated humanely because every human being possesses inalienable dignity. Among its irrevocable directives, the first and foremost is the commitment to a culture of non-violence and respect for life. It declares that no people, no State, no race, no religion has the right to hate, to discriminate against, to 'cleanse', to exile, much less to liquidate a 'foreign' minority which is different in behaviour or holds different beliefs. It lays down that all human conflicts should be resolved without violence within a framework of justice. It calls for universal disarmament. It recommends that young people must learn the culture of non-violence both at home and at school. It says that a human person is infinitely precious and must be unconditionally protected and, likewise, lives of animals and plants which inhabit this planet with us deserve protection, preservation and care. First, it declares that we are all interdependent together in this cosmos and each one of us depends on the welfare of all. Secondly, it calls for a culture of solidarity and just economic order. Thirdly, it calls for a commitment to a culture of tolerance and a life of truthfulness. Fourthly, it calls for a commitment to a culture of equal rights and partnership between men and women. The premise of the Declaration is that on the foundations of these commitments, a new consciousness of ethical responsibility can be mobilised for the creation of a new and humane global community of peoples of different nationalities, origins, ideologies and faiths living together in harmony.

The 1993 Parliament of World's Religions has a significance far beyond the commemoration of a momentous event which happened a hundred years ago. It represents the compelling relevance of an ecumenical approach to life in our global village in our age and time and which is marked by emerging patterns of multi-cultural pluralism. Its significance also lies in the readiness of the World's Religions to dialogue and work together in creating a common ethical framework and to declare themselves against isolation, exclusivism, fanaticism and intolerance.

A hundred years ago, on 11 September 1893, Charles Carol Bonney had said in the opening address to the Parliament of World's Religions, 'The very basis of our convocation is the idea that the representatives of each religion sincerely believe it is the truest and the best of all.' In 1993, delegations of different religious persuasions would have had no difficulty in agreeing with Mahatma Gandhi who said that various religions were as leaves of a tree which might seem different but at the trunk they were one. Perhaps, the most significant contribution of the Parliament of World's Religions is in the emphasis on the moral and spiritual roots of the human civilisation.

V

I would conclude my tale of three cities with the thought that although the three cities are far-flung, they belong together in the contemporary blueprint of new world order. There is a remarkable coherence of concentricity in the concerns represented by the three cities. All three of them have a common core. That common core is the cluster of basic values of humanity manifested in the human instinct for survival, in the human need for growth and development, in the human aspiration for dignity, in human rights and obligations, and in ethical responsibility and spiritual fulfilment. The tale of each city is therefore a tale of all three cities as well. The UN Secretary-General Mr Boutros Boutros Ghali pointed out in his 1992 Report on the Work of the United Nations Organisation, 'Human Rights are an essential component of sustainable development; sustainable development is not possible without respect for Human Rights.' One might add that a global universal human ethic, proclaimed in Chicago, encompasses both sustainable development and human rights. The tale of Rio is thus repeated in Vienna and both of them are retold in Chicago. In the ultimate analysis, each one of the cities of humankind is cast in the image of the City of God with people living and striving together in harmony and unflinching quest of peace and justice, or as the great Indian poet Tagore put it:

> Where the mind is without fear and the head is held high;
> Where knowledge is free;
> Where the world has not been broken up into fragments by
>   narrow domestic walls;
> Where words come out from the depth of truth;
> Where tireless striving stretches its arms towards perfection;
> Where the clear stream of reason has not lost its way into the
>   dreary desert sand of dead habit;
> Where the mind is led forward by thee into ever-widening
>   thought and action –
> Into that heaven of freedom, my Father, let my country awake.*

Will this dream ever come true? Will my tale have a happy ending? Yes, if men and women grow in moral stature. Otherwise, as Edwin Markham put it:

> Why build these cities glorious
> If man unbuilded goes?
> In vain we build the world, unless
> The builder also grows.†

---

* Rabindranath Tagore, *Gitanjali* xxxv
† Edwin Markham, *Man-Making* (1920)

Printed in the United States
By Bookmasters